SHARK ATTACK
and OTHER MISHAPS

ALSO BY PELLER MARION

Crisis Proof Your Career   Birch Lane Press, 1993

Career Tune Up   Artemis Arts Library, 2005

Searching for the G Spot   Artemis Arts Library, 2005

Shopping Lessons   Artemis Arts Library, 2004

SHARK ATTACK
and OTHER MISHAPS

PELLER MARION

ARTEMIS ARTS LIBRARY
San Francisco, California

ISBN: 978-0-9746927-4-6

Mixed media cover art, *Intimate Encounter* by Peller Marion

Book and cover design by Jeremy Thornton, jftdesign.com

ARTEMIS ARTS LIBRARY
San Francisco, California

artemisartslibrary.com

Let me fall if I must fall,
The one I will become will
catch me.
–The Baal Shem Tov

———◦———

This book is for Ron Tilden,
my husband

Acknowledgements

My friends at Tiburon Community
Congregational Church, our
Writing From The Heart group,

O'Hanlon Center for the Arts
in Mill Valley, California,

The Mermaids at Harbor Point,
Elsa Dixon, and Jacob Liberman,
my deepest appreciation.

Contents

1. Shark Attack 1

2. Alone in the Ocean 3

3. The Perfect Vacation 7

4. Maui Mermaids 13

5. The Night Before 19

6. The Drifters 25

7. Panic in the Moment 29

8. Paramedics on the Beach 33

9. Emergency Room 39

10. The Reporters 45

11. Remembering Unsafe Places 53

12. Wanting My Mother 59

13. A Visit from a Hawaiian Shaman 67

14. Remembering Botswana 73

15. Another Encounter – Breast Cancer 79

16. Breast Cancer – Redux 87

17. Remembering the Death of a Friend 95

18. Dread & Marriage Theory 101

19. Heart Surgery 109

20. Coping 121

21. The Gardener 131

22. Time for Reflection 139

23. Saying Goodbye 143

24. Mother Maui 145

1. Shark Attack

ONE OUT OF NINETY-EIGHT MILLION PEOPLE are attacked by a shark. I was one of them.

One morning in May, as I swam offshore in Maui, the water sparkled with unusual clarity, and I was hoping—outfitted in my goggles, snorkel, and flippers—that I'd encounter some green sea turtles. They had been coming closer to shore in the last few days and bobbed to the surface for several seconds to gaze glassy-eyed at me before they submerged again. Sometimes I'd follow one farther out to the rock. Friends called the spot "The Airport," because the turtles gathered there like grounded planes at their terminal gates.

It was often hard to find the exact location of "The Airport," but I'd follow an older, slower turtle—six or eight feet in diameter—and eventually she would lead me back to an underwater giant piece of rock where hundreds of turtles were all facing into the coral outcroppings, eating the green algae that formed on the crevices. Different size turtles came home to this place and were resting layer upon layer. Some had barnacles on their soft, fleshy necks, others had remnants of cruel encounters with fishing lines and hooks, and some were babies, lighter in color and texture.

I lay on my stomach above them for hours, gazing at the scene below me as they moved at a glacial pace until my body felt waterlogged or I became bored. Each encounter with a turtle was different. Some saw me, dove down, and then popped up in front of me, staring curiously before they disappeared again. Some hung around, spying on me from a safe distance—like my cat did at home, peering around a corner or hiding behind the bed—while other turtles I encountered fled quickly. They were like people, each with distinct personalities: some social, some asocial and quirky.

The water and weather could change very quickly in the ocean, and I found myself at times battling unforeseen currents, swells, or struggling in a riptide that had caught me unaware. And unlike lap swimming in a pool, I had to stay alert. It was the law of the ocean.

I had been swimming for a half an hour when I felt a razor-sharp pain shoot through my torso, like I had been hit by a bolt of lightning. Something had come up behind me and clamped onto my right leg. Its teeth broke my skin and cut through it like it was biting into a marshmallow. It wouldn't let go. It held onto me and hurled me forward with a fury, shooting me underwater at lightning speed. Finally it let go, and I was inches away from the side of the shark's open mouth, I caught sight of its rows of pointed teeth. It stared at me with dead eyes. At first, I had thought the creature in the water was a large sea turtle, but my new swim fin popped off, and it went flying over the swells. Then I saw a wall of gray. I was face to face with a raging tiger shark the size of, and the power of, a freight train. My mind registered: I am food. I could die here.

Hard and fast, I kicked my leg free, and desperately turned to swim away, but where there had been clear water, now there was a massive silvery body with no beginning or end. With that kick, I sensed I was now along the side of the shark. Treading in thirty feet of water, I was in a wildness I'd never known. The shark's force struck me to my core—my body was no longer mine. The sea had reached out and thrust me into its mysterious depths. For a moment, I lost all my will. I felt an old feeling from childhood—a despair when my father overpowered me in a rage.

With my head still underwater, I saw my blood around me. Salt water flooded my nose, mouth, and seeped under my goggles. I frantically broke the surface, gasped for air, turned, and swam—flailing frantically—and started to swim swiftly toward shore, certain that the shark was coming after me, swift and sure.

My right leg didn't feel like it belonged to me anymore. Strangely, the salt water felt cool and pleasant on my limb, but I knew that something awful had happened. I also knew that if I stopped and looked at it I'd panic.

My thoughts were chaotic, and fast. Something had reached inside me and forcibly informed me that I no longer had a free pass. Suddenly I was very awake and began swimming slowly and deliberately, talking myself out of succumbing to the fear that filled my belly. I thought, "You can't outswim the shark. If it wants you, it'll come after you. Don't drown yourself with panic."

My thoughts raced. Images rushed past me in flashes. In my mind's eye, I saw my head torn from my body—my mind still working while my severed torso pushed past me, caught in the swells. Now, in the ocean, blood pooled to the surface as I desperately swam toward shore.

2. Alone in the Ocean

A COUPLE OF YEARS BEFORE, my husband and I had walked on the beach at dusk and seen a photo posted on a tree about a man my age who'd gone out for an evening swim and never returned.

When we'd inquired, the property manager had told us that they'd found the man's towel, wallet, and watch tucked behind a bush near the shore. I remember wondering what would I have done if my husband hadn't returned from a swim in the ocean. At first, I would imagine that he—the consummate conversationalist—had run into an old Maui friend, and would wander home with his head full of current island gossip. Often on his way home at the end of a day, he'd call me from his cell phone, and I'd hear excitement in his voice. "I can't wait to tell you a juicy tidbit of gossip I heard."

"Tell me now."

"No, it's better to tell you in person. I want to see your face when I tell you."

But the scenario could go a different way. After several hours without hearing from him, I know I'd be frantic. I'd run down to the beach, I'd ask everyone I saw, I'd go mental, and finally—in despair—I'd call the police. I'm sure he'd walk in the door about then, claiming he'd lost track of time.

I wondered—*what would be his first thought if I didn't return that morning?* He was a bit more laid-back than I was about things like this. I'd been known to wander off window-shopping, only to wander back a short time later. Yet, I was more predictable in my movements, and always told him where I was going and when I'd be back. If I was late, I'd always call. It seemed to me his early internal alert system would be slower to activate—but once it did, he'd be out looking for me.

Every day on our Maui vacations, I swam for an hour or more parallel to the shore, just outside the rocks that softened the breaking waves and made a trough. Finally, exhausted, I felt the pleasure of my body as it drifted back to the beach.

Early that morning I announced, "I've got to get an edge on the day," to my husband, hoping he would hear and want to join me, but he rolled over and went back to sleep. I opened the curtain and peered out. I already knew I couldn't get him in the ocean at that time of morning. He claimed that some people were floaters, and others were sinkers. He claimed he had more muscle and less body fat, so that made him a sinker. He'd jump in the surf and take a quick dip, but that was all.

At that time of day, I knew the beach would be fairly empty. Perhaps I'd see one or two die-hard swimmers freestyling in the same channel we carved out from Mana Kai to Ulua Beach — quite a stretch round-trip.

Being alone in the ocean had its own magic. It was dangerous, frightening, and expansive. Past the sounds of the booming surf, there was a silence buffered by the sounds of wind and restless swells. The salt water was a safety net that kept me from sinking and gave me comfort, like lying in the hands of God. And because I was a visitor here, unlike the green turtles that rose to the surface every so often to breathe, I couldn't stay forever.

There was a surfer that I'd read about once, whose arms were caught in a shark's mouth. Instead of fighting for his life, and because the shark was holding him under water as he propelled forward out to sea, he'd given up, and he was carried far out, tethered to the underbelly of the animal. It was only when friends in a Zodiac saw him that he was rescued. Would I have an energy reserve to save myself, or drop into helplessness like the surfer?

From past adventures, I remembered all the ocean's sudden, dark moods when I'd been with some good swimmers beside me. Once, we treaded ten-foot swells in the harsh waters of La Parouse, while two of us steadied my friend who took a fishhook out of the mouth of an enormous green sea turtle. At first the turtle flailed and fought us, but suddenly the turtle stilled itself, as if knowing we were helping him to stay alive. Another time, I got myself out of a riptide. No one had spoken of riptides, currents, or shark attacks on this part of the island in the twenty years I'd been an open ocean swimmer and swam each morning for miles in Maui waters.

I never could get over the sea with its many moods, glass-smooth and stone-rough, at certain times wondrously open and at others tightly inscrutable, sometimes a weak blue so clear that you could see straight down to the puffer fish hiding in the crevices inside the coral, looking spiked and expectant. And then there was an impenetrable Prussian blue — the color of my favorite oil pastel — as my eye traveled into the depths of the water.

There were the sensations of swimming: Using my torso to power my swim, not my arms or legs, I could swim for miles and barely splash on the surface of the water. A friend and I watched how fish swim effortlessly.

"Fish don't have necks, so they move as one unit. To swim like a fish, you must move from one side to the other, using your core as your engine and letting your legs follow the rhythm originating from your hips—not pulling with your arms, but gliding to get the most out of each stroke," a friend said. I imagined being a mermaid when I swam, as if my home were in the water. The rhythm was mesmerizing after a while, but I was warned that I always had to stay alert to changes in the ocean.

Fulton, a Maui friend, told us how years before he was eating dinner at a restaurant across the street from the ocean on the road to Lahaina and suddenly found himself and other diners watching a shark devour a female swimmer while her friend swam frantically to shore for help that came too late. Shark attacks in Maui seemed rare, sudden, and often deadly.

3. The Perfect Vacation

IN 1989, WE CAME TO MAUI FOR THE FIRST TIME on a recommendation from a friend of Ron's at Esalen Institute in Big Sur, where I led workshops.

"My ex-boyfriend is a horse whisperer in Maui. He owns fourteen horses and a real working ranch. He takes people out on horseback rides," she said.

This image of horses and beaches ignited my husband's imagination. Soon after, we headed to Maui on a non-stop flight for the perfect vacation.

On the way to the San Francisco airport to fly out, Ron told the taxi driver, "I have to knock out my wife, throw her in a sack, and drag her to the airport just to get her to take a vacation."

I was bleary-eyed from a sleepless night because of anxiety and excitement. Fog and mist rose up, shrouding us as we crossed the Golden Gate Bridge. Steel girders disappeared, then reappeared in the fog. Once on the plane, it was magical to head into the rising sun at six o'clock in the morning on a non-stop flight out of San Francisco airport. It was hard to image that in five hours we'd be enveloped in heat, humidity, and sun.

The night before I had packed an extra bag of paperback books, my journal, favorite pens, and my sketch pad. I lived in dread that I'd be caught up short without anything to do, afraid I'd be bored, and being in the present wasn't all that absorbing. Maybe there would be too much present time to fill all that space. I needed self-inflicted projects.

I recognized that this was something I'd seen my mother do all my life. Yet, I worked so hard not to be like my mother — driven and a real black-and-white thinker — or to resemble my mother, who was short and stocky, but after menopause, my waist had thickened, my face broadened, and people who knew both of us often commented that I was the spitting image of her. Even my phone voice sounded like hers. No matter how little I ate, and no matter how much I exercised, I couldn't get away from my genetic legacy.

The truth I carried inside me was that it wasn't so hard to be like my workaholic and opinionated mother. I actually was beginning to like and understand her as a woman. Of course, it was all in my head — but she was my touchstone, after all.

Flying to Maui, hour after hour, we crossed the blue expanse of ocean, until suddenly a verdant landscape unfolded before us. Heading west, time went backwards by three hours, and we would arrive for breakfast.

We gazed below at the three hundred and sixty-degree vista spread before us. Everything was alive with interest. The sun was brilliant and unrelenting over Prussian blue mountains and a cerulean ocean. Lush green-and-yellow fields of pineapple and sugar cane were outlined by mango orchards. They looked like colorful postage stamps from the air. The hills rolled down to the beach, and I could see Wailea, where we were staying.

As we stepped off the plane in Kahului, the humidity overpowered us, and the air was filled with sweet fragrances from the bright yellow poinciana, red plumeria, and lavender jacaranda trees, carried along by the light and mist in the air. The airport terminal building, unlike airports on the mainland, had no windows. It was open to the morning breeze.

The first couple of days, I felt drugged and jetlagged — like a boiled chicken. The temperature rose to ninety-eight degrees, and the humidity stayed at eighty-six. In the outdoor mall, stores like Versace, Tiffany, and Saks Fifth Avenue welcomed herds of tourists window-shopping and moving like sleepwalkers in the heat with lobster red skin, husbands with newly bought Tommy Bahama short sleeve shirts concealing their paunches, women and kids sporting lounge wear and licking Lampert's ice cream cones.

Haleakala rose out of the island like a strange apparition. It was startling any time of day. Its changing moods were like the ocean beneath its feet. The sunlight made shadows on the dark lava that had flowed and then cooled down its southern sides into the sea.

At the hotel, I had the outdoor Jacuzzi all to myself. The first several nights I awoke to the stillness and the silence during some mysterious moments when I imagined Mother Maui inhaling and then slowly exhaling, leaving a long pause at the top of her breath. Then I heard the waves softly lap against the shore. In the middle of the night, when my head hit the pillow, I thought of Dolly, our cat back in Mill Valley, purring in my ear as I dropped off to a deep dreamless sleep. I felt spacy throughout the day, not knowing what to do with myself. I never opened my bag of books. There was something about the subtropics that took all the striving out of me, like sitting in a hot sauna, or having the flu. I felt my body in a way I didn't like: it was thick and dull and clumsy. Usually I was a brain and a spinal cord, but here in the subtropics I couldn't help being in my body. The dizzying heat pressed inward, begging my body for attention.

In the morning hours, it seemed like every snowbird invaded the beach. Faces changed each day. There were mothers, fathers, kids, and babies from the Midwest. I didn't see that many older people. Where were they hiding?

Ron didn't hesitate to call Flynn, the horse whisperer, and book a ride in the upcountry. Flynn gave me a gentle old horse and told me to hang on no matter what. I'm never one to mess with—much less ride—anything bigger than me, so I proceeded with caution.

Flynn and Ron hit it off immediately, and Flynn invited us to his friend's birthday party the following night. We drove up to Wes and Natalie's home in Ulapalakua. The compound was set back from a rural highway, up a dirt road—the house was one story with a thatched, sloping roof, lots of glass doors and verandas. This was the way I imagined a real Maui home—with hills and pasture surrounding the property.

Wes greeted us, and invited us into a great room. From there we saw a wraparound view of Maui. It was like standing in a postcard you would send home. Spread out below us was a hallucinatory-like landscape of waterfalls, gorges, and clouds that floated by, at times obscuring the volcano.

Everyone seemed to know each other already. Marvin and Della, Jake, and Flynn and Aurora, and Fuzzy and Gina all made us feel like we had known them for years.

A large man in a white silk suit and a panama hat came out onto the deck, cutting a figure of formidable importance. He looked like a pimp or a drug dealer—very out of place in this relaxed setting with casually dressed guests. He reached under his hat and threw a baggie filled with white powder onto the picnic table.

"I thought you might need this," he said to Wes, who took it off the table in a good-natured way. The man made a gesture toward Ron, holding his left nostril closed while he mimicked sniffing the powdered-filled baggie with his right nostril. Everyone joined in the laughter. What had we gotten ourselves into by coming here?

We became the newest entertainment in Maui. We carried a certain cachet and excitement on this small, insular island community. It felt like a small town.

So began our adventure with an unlikely group of people.

I was finding that one of the benefits of aging was that if you knew your limits, and you could fast-track the consequences of any decision before you fell flat on your face or got sick, you would be okay. Well, sometimes.

Our new friend with the white powder, Wes, said, "No matter how far you drive in Maui, you end up back again where you started by sundown."

Wes and Flynn became our adventure guides for the next several decades.

Life was becoming an accumulation of experiences and the consequences of the choices we've made. A bittersweet feeling would wash over me sometimes when I thought about how life had used us up. I saw that so clearly in my friends — and felt it in myself.

When I thought of living in Maui, I felt excitement, followed by sensation of claustrophobia. How long would it take me to get island fever when I experienced the fact that there were minimal distractions, and you took yourself wherever you went? "It's kinda like life," I joked.

Sometimes, back in California, I was so consumed by my own bad thoughts and self-recriminations that I thought of checking into a hermitage or convent down near Big Sur. You know — those places where a humble woman shuffles to the main gate to let you in late at night, greets you, and carries your bags inside to your room. I imagined that I'd be given a small room with no windows, a cot, and a slot in the door where the food tray would be passed through twice a day. I pictured going there to write or meditate. My fear was that after several days of solitude and writer's block, the humble servant would see the uneaten food, open the door, and find me dead on the floor. An autopsy would reveal no known cause of death.

"She probably died of her own bad thoughts," friends would finally conclude.

At the party, we were standing out on the deck listening to Della and Marvin talk about the essential oil and lotion business that they owned and that was still in its infant stages of development. Could people really make a living on this island, I wondered? If they could, maybe we could, too.

That evening, we met all the people who would become major figures in our Maui life for the next twenty-five years. We had gotten in with a zany, post hippie, ex-drug dealing crowd of people. As a wanna-be sociologist, and self-styled profiler, I discovered that there were other groups and subsets of groups on the island: the golf crowd, the surfer crowd, the newly rich from the Midwest, and the transplants from California that Maui people called the *Pineapple Express*. The locals called us "Haoles" — a name for most white people born and raised on the mainland.

Wes gave us the lowdown on the island and his friends.

"We all lived in Florida in the sixties. I met these guys because they were friends with Natalie. They were all dealing drugs. Fuzzy's dad owned a popular outdoor food stand in Boston called Fuzzy's Beef. Gina, his girlfriend and an airline hostess, used her job—as some women did at that time—to fly drugs from Florida to Boston. Flynn had a trust fund, and Jake was the only one with a real job—as a financial advisor."

Now I had an idea of where many of the hippies had gone after the sixties. They dropped out, tuned in, and turned on in Maui. They became pot farmers, horse whisperers, health-food store owners, self-styled gurus, and essential oil sales people. Much later, some became real estate agents.

Natalie became a real estate agent. She showed me several condos and homes in Maui Meadows and Wailea that were for sale. She had a habit of chatting absentmindedly while driving and making left hand turns into oncoming cars. In fact, that is how she ended up in a crippling car accident years later that caused her decline and death.

We were so enamored with the island that Ron and I talked about buying a house there. We had seen one right on the beach with a burnished front gate that made it look like a compound. He called it our "mansionette." Only a few years later, the shark attack would occur just a couple of hundred yards from the house we never bought. In those early days of excitement, why had we changed our minds?

We had gotten in with a group of people in their fifties in the twenty-first century, thirty years after People's Park, the Chicago Eight, and marches in Selma. These people had become fathers, mothers wearing bras with badly behaving children, and grandparents with several grandchildren. They looked normal, but their stories embodied a drifting life with arbitrary decisions.

On the other hand, I always thought that my life would be free of bumps in the road after I reached fifty. I thought it would be a free ride after I cut back my work. Was that a way to reassure myself? After all, my parents retired to a quiet respite in New Jersey, living comfortably with no major illnesses. They traveled and took vacations. I thought we'd settle into a similar lifestyle.

That evening, we watched the red ball of fire descend into the ocean, danced to live music, ate mangos, papayas, raw tuna, drank too much wine, smoked dope, and pretended we were young again—legends in our own minds.

4. Maui Mermaids

OUR LIVES SEEMED FILTERED through our illusions. We told ourselves a story about our lives to feel good about ourselves. And as we got older, people we loved died, slipped away, or moved, and there were fewer people to corroborate the story that we marketed — the story that we'd been peddling of our successes and achievements. I didn't realize then that strangers would look at me and see a wrinkled, older woman and be unable to imagine anything more.

Sometimes I imagined wearing a lanyard around my neck with a laminated photo of how I looked in my best decade — probably when I was twenty-eight years old.

Not by accident, Ron and I decided that we were going to spend more time in Maui. After a few visits, we rented a three-bedroom home in old Makena right on the water near the old Hawaiian Church. At night, we were lulled to sleep by the waves that crashed up against the rocks outside. In the morning, the fragrance of the moist earth woke us and the cardinals sang their hearts out, sounding like rusty swings in the nearby trees. Hummingbirds frantically buzzed the branches that were weighed down with mangos outside the living room window, and barn sparrows made their nest in a branch by the kitchen. We were looking for our tribe, our family. Tired of working so hard, we wanted out of the rat race that we had jumped into years before, and now we saw there was more to life. We could relax more, work less, and have a good time.

While Flynn was taking us on horse riding trips, and building his life with his young wife, another chapter of life was unfolding for us.

One of the unexpected gifts of aging is that if you are curious about people and their stories, you are there when the final chapters of their lives unfold. I began to see how their choices and their personalities informed them as we all slipped into the last third of our lives. In retrospect, it became that way with many of our friends in Maui.

Yet here was a place that could so easily throw one off balance. We knew that, but we felt untouched. Sure, there were hurricanes, volcanoes, drownings, and flash floods, but in comparison to everyday mainland hassles, the pace of life here seemed slow and easy.

Surprisingly for paradise, the weather could become unsettled, a wind could blow up by midmorning, and then everyone grabbed their beach towels and scurried off the beach.

"Boy, this wasn't in the brochure," I heard one tourist say to his wife as he grabbed his water sport toys and ran for cover. "Call the kids and get them out of the water. Get them out of the pool."

Suddenly, it began raining buckets, and thunder and lightning rampaged across the sky, the vast ocean framing the whole experience. The mood crept into everyone's psyches. Tourists sat in disbelief, sipping their umbrella drinks on their covered lanais and watching the skies open as the drama unfolded. There was a surreal quality to the scene—like watching an adventure movie.

Wes said, "The sea is angry today. No one could last an hour out there."

The smell of the ocean was so strong that I could almost gulp it off the breeze. Waves broke against the rocks in front of our rental house, and then the waves sucked the water down again into the coral beds.

"It smells like fish poop," I joked.

Wes said, "It's called fish guano, dearie."

In the distance, one could see the vast gray expanse and hear the ocean's constant roar. There wasn't a day that went by when I wouldn't read of swimmers near drowning, flailing to no avail when their scuba device failed, or drowning in flash floods. There was a force behind the scenes where nature felt like it was always beside you, informing you or warning you, if you just listened carefully enough. FOX or CNN news from the mainland felt like constant unreal entertainment. It didn't feel relevant to us here on an island that was twenty-five hundred miles from the mainland. Life was buoyant on Mother Maui.

And because of this, our excitement was building, and everyone and everything was alive with interest. We had been captives of our own making in the world of corporate consulting, and now we had found something rich and vital, and we both wanted to uncover more.

Yet I should have listened to other, subtler voices. One night, I dreamed that I was shopping and bought a skimpy taffeta cocktail dress that was low-cut, with spaghetti straps. I wore it out onto the beach and people stared at me. Then I dove deep into the ocean and I came up wearing a dark veil and a black, floor-length dress that covered every part of me—my arms, my legs, and even my neck, like funeral attire—as I walked out of the surf. Was that a prescient moment for the events that would unfold? How had I dismissed a dream that was so clearly there to be seen?

In the early days of being on Maui, I fell in with a group of women around my age who called themselves The Maui Mermaids. Early each morning, I got a call from one of them letting me know the wind, surf conditions, and where to meet. I bounced out of bed, got my gear and off I went for several hours. The group consisted of Aurora, who gave massages to tourists at the hotels that dotted the beach, Natalie, who got blood transfusions in London on an annual basis because she had HIV (I think she told us she had met Keith Richards on one of her clinic trips), and Gina, a former rock group singer, who had been the vocalist with Neil Young (or was it Neil Diamond?). Anyway, that was her big claim to fame.

I opened the curtain and peered out. At eight in the morning, I knew the beach would be fairly empty. Perhaps I'd see one or two die-hard swimmers freestyling in the same channel we carved out from Mana Kai to the Ahihi Beach—a twelve-mile stretch round-trip.

In the early morning, we met past the rocks at Ahihi Bay. It was a small area near a hexagon-shaped house where the coastline was just becoming rugged. Aurora wore her mermaid costume—a pearlescent rash guard, florescent cap, and silvery tights.

The others dressed in fish-like costumes. They were all as lithe as eels. Natalie headed the pack. You couldn't harness her liveliness. It could provide electricity to a whole village. I was lucky if I got there on time and had my bathing suit on under my sundress because I was a late sleeper. We entered the water together and swam out as far as we could. I oriented myself and looked back at the shore. Occasionally, I saw a person fishing off the rocks. I dove under and looked up, feeling my weightlessness and agelessness. I came to the surface. I wasn't a man or a woman, and I wasn't defined by the way I looked or what I did. I was bone, muscle, and movement. All my thoughts were dulled by the immediacy of the moment. I was excited. I was scared. I kicked, rotated my arms, breathed, dipping my face into the warm water, coming up for air, cutting through the water, and keeping up with these master swimmers. Directly beneath us were vast arrays of fish: schools of yellow tangs, Moorish idols, ornate wrasses, and red parrotfish. Not just one fish, but schools of fish darted past, swimming beneath our legs, and were followed by more schools of entirely different kinds of fish. The rays of light reflected off the coral, making moving patterns of colors beneath us.

That morning, I felt like Honey Ryder, played by Ursula Andress, in the beach scene in the movie *Dr. No*. Unlike me, these other Maui Mermaid gals went swimming every day. Growing up in the suburbs after World War II on the East Coast, I had never had any Huck Finn adventures that moved my soul, or deepened my trust in my body. But here, in the water, my body felt stirrings I'd never felt before—I was strong and capable. The magic of the ocean: I was something special here, and I was nobody here. I had to stay alert to the mercurial ocean and all its unpredictability.

Later that morning, we were met by Wes, the husband of Natalie, who had a Zodiac. He cranked the engine and circled us with the rubber boat. We piled in, then he motored out farther. At one point, I thought we were headed to Japan. Finally, Wes stalled the Zodiac and pointed to a spot several hundred yards from us. A shiny object popped out of the water for a moment.

"It's a bottlenose dolphin. Jump in, jump in!" yelled Wes.

Immediately, we all flung our bodies off the boat and left the Zodiac bobbing in the water, and I followed the women who swam away. In minutes, hundreds of huge, silvery creatures were swarming around us in forty feet of water. As far as my eyes could see, there were dolphins. Then, as if hearing a dog whistle, the dolphins turned in a pack, in unison, and darted off. They were gone. The water was clear and still. Several seconds later, as if they had regrouped under the surface, they swiftly returned in a pack. There must have been hundreds of large, silver torpedo-headed dolphins headed straight towards us. As they got closer to us, they suddenly—as if by some silent signal—synchronized and veered off, keeping their distance. This went on for almost an hour. Later, Wes pointed his oar to where they were in the water ahead of us now, and we frantically swam out to meet them again and again. This time when they saw us, they regrouped and swam toward us in their pack, an army of silvery creatures—mysterious, mystical. At first and for a split second, I worried that they were going to attack us, but the three other women didn't flinch and held their places, so I did, too. When the dolphins got within several yards, they veered off again, but this time they came a lot closer. At one point, I felt the water shift, like a breeze had come up, and several brushed past my skin, grazing my legs as if they were petting me.

Maybe that's why I'd been painting dimly-lit, watery worlds. It was a way of recording in metaphor images of my own remembered waterscapes. I wanted to see what would float up to my consciousness as I painted underwater creatures—dark, big predators. I thought they were whales that breached as we floated far out in our Zodiac, or bottlenose dolphins flipping high in the air in the wake of the boat. Who would have thought what was to come? Who would have thought what they really were?

I have heard it said that survivors look back and wonder if they saw omens or if they missed something. Did I miss a message in a dream I'd had? Did I miss a message in the paintings I'd made?

Finally, Wes turned his Zodiac around and headed toward shore, leaving us. We decided to swim out to a spot called "The Aquarium." Usually locals found it by looking for a cracked boulder down a dirt road in the lava fields and following a worn unmarked footpath, but in the ocean we could find it faster by following the coastal outcroppings until we saw the cove. The out-of-the-way cove was surrounded by cliffs on three sides, and at the foot of the cliffs lay a deep pool of seawater that was fed by the incoming tide. The sound of the tide crashing over the rocks seemed treacherous, so we took turns being propelled by the waves to get into "The Aquarium." One by one, we made it over the rocky opening, riding over the crashing waves into the pool. The roar of the waves crashing over the rocks was deafening, so we called out to one another once we jumped into and rode the surf. Once inside the pool, there were cliff walls that had small openings, like shelves in a library, and inside each of these openings were thousands of schools of little fish: longnose butterflyfish, lionfish, yellowtail wrasse, and Picasso triggerfish were only a few that Aurora called by name. It seemed like a universe unto itself — untouched, and it was mesmerizing to swim into what felt like a gigantic fishbowl. I could understand when someone used the term bird's-eye view. In this space, it felt like I was having a fish's-eye view of the water. It felt like a place untouched and sacred that only few people had ever visited.

On the way back, with the shore still off in the distance, Aurora screamed. I spun around and saw parts of her face and hair covered under a mass of a gelatinous sea life. Some tentacles reached down across her face, so that her eyes peered out in terror. It appeared that sitting on the top of her head was a slimy sack the size of a cat. She screamed at the top of her lungs.

"It's stinging me, it's stinging me! Help me! Get it off me."

She kept grabbing at her hair and face.

At first, I didn't know what had happened to her. What was this goopy, disgusting mass on her face? Then Natalie yelled, "Swim to shore, swim to shore!" Aurora was struggling with one hand pulling at the tentacles, and with the other arm grabbing at the water, making paddling movements but hardly gaining any forward motion.

We circled around her while treading water, grabbing at the tentacles of the creature without getting caught by them ourselves. They felt slippery, clinging, and unmanageable. The creature's main body was a ball of gelatinous ooze with tentacles, and I had to force myself to help her.

Natalie yelled, "It's a Portuguese man-of-war!"

The way Aurora flailed, the words "man-of-war," and the swells made my stomach roil with seasickness. I let go and turned my back to the women. I vomited into the water, and it was swept away with a swell and disappeared a distance away. Then, along with the others, I swam back and tried to pull the tentacles out of Aurora's hair while treading water. She was yelling in pain the whole time, and we were yelling at her, "Calm down, calm down."

Gina, who was the strongest swimmer, got in front of Aurora, rolled her onto her back, and dragged her to the shore, while we pushed and trailed from behind. Meanwhile, we pulled, grabbed, and tore at the remaining tentacles. The beach was empty at that time of the morning. Once on shore, we continued pulling the tentacles out of her tangled long hair as she moaned and screamed in pain.

"Grab the sac and pull it off of her," Gina yelled.

I hesitated.

"Grab it, damn you!" she shouted at me. I wasn't working fast enough.

I grabbed the core of the creature from where the tentacles originated and yanked hard. The blob came off Aurora's head with a loud, squishy, sucking sound, and with it, most of the tentacles. My stomach was in knots. Gina found a large, concave shell, pulled the bottom of her bathing suit to one side, squatted and peed into it. Then she poured the urine over the red welts on Aurora's face and upper arm, using her hand to smear it around the welts. Aurora fought angrily.

"Stop it, stop it, you bitch."

Gina ignored her screams and pointed to me. "We need more."

Gina tossed me the shell and I gingerly scrambled over some lava, feeling queasy again. I pulled my one-piece bathing suit aside to squat and pee into the shell.

Soon, Aurora calmed down and lay on the beach, exhausted. She closed her eyes while we dried our bodies on the warm lava and sand. We had given everything over to heart, blood, muscle, and bone. We sat there in silence for quite a while, facing the water, watching the waves roll in and out on the beach and the sun rising higher in the morning sky. I never thought for a moment that the ocean held an even bigger surprise for me alone.

5. The Night Before

MONTHS LATER, I thought about this episode and how it puzzled me. It had always felt like there was a mysterious, unseen presence beckoning. This presence was something I feared but was also forced to open up to. It was vigilant and foreboding. I'm a woman in a small body, and I've always been anxious about my safety. Why did the shark attack me? Why now? What did this episode mean?

We are all broken, but broken in different ways. My way of getting broken was living with a rage-oholic mother, an emotionally frozen father, and a brother who might erupt unpredictably. It made me afraid of everything — yet I was always challenging my fear.

There have been many puzzling events in my life. Often they made me ask major questions over and over again. Each time, the journey involved ever increasing depth and circularity. This feeling was a longing for the answers to the questions — the excitement about the future and the possibilities — that were in store for me. Was this shark attack a random act, or did it have some meaning?

I was a latchkey child growing up in the fifties, when mothers stayed at home and made their children cucumber and mayonnaise sandwiches on white bread with the crust cut off. I came home to an empty house, made my tuna sandwich, and waited anxiously for my mom. I was brought up not to ask for help, expecting no one to give it. And often they didn't. As the youngest child of two working parents, I had to learn how to fight my own battles. There was always a foreboding that my mother wouldn't return, or that some intruder would be in the house when I opened the door, and this led me unknowingly later on to confront my fears and overcome them. Swimming was one such fear.

Every day as an adolescent, I walked through the empty high school auditorium, which was a shortcut from the front of the building to the back for my last-period French class. And every day, I'd look over my shoulder at the Thomas wall clock, mounted high above the door, to see how much time was left. I was counting down the months, days, hours, and minutes until my formal education was over and my real life would begin. Goodbye to

Friday assemblies, the Pledge of Allegiance to the Flag of The United States of America, the Lord's Prayer, and the John Phillip Sousa marching song that accompanied us to find our row and our seat on assembly day. Goodbye to Mrs. Whiteskill's opening remarks and announcements. And no more coming home to an empty house. My expansive life — reckless, and full of possibilities — lay ahead.

During that period of my life, I'd lie awake at night and listen to the faraway sounds on the radio: Wheeling, West Virginia came in reedy with the soft voice of Loretta Lynn or sometimes Bobby Blue Bland. Often KWOR out of New York: Wolfman Jack and a raspy voice of a young, unknown singer, Bob Dylan, singing "Mr. Tambourine Man."

Manhattan — a mere twenty miles northwest across Irvington, past Newark Airport, Secaucus, over the Pulanski Skyway, and through the Holland Tunnel — seemed as far away as the moon to me.

Yet, little did I know that one song would follow me for decades across continents, through relationships, careers, and now here to Maui.

And I later wondered — where had the eighteen-foot tiger shark been the night before it seized my leg in the waters off Maui?

My husband Ron and I had been at a party the night before the attack. It was a benefit for our friend Natalie's disadvantaged children's camp, where she was a volunteer. Over the years, we had developed friendships with many couples who had lived on the island since the mid-sixties. They all had stories to tell about easy island living back then, and how they had found their niches over the last four and a half decades. These were people I would have called hippies, dopers, or surfer types back in the sixties. They had all gravitated to the islands then, and stayed. They were middle class and late middle aged now. No longer were these friends reckless and wild as we'd all been in the sixties, but had been absorbed into island life: a restaurateur, a naturalist at The Maui Ocean Center, an owner of a kayak company, an owner of a horse ranch, and a well-known architect.

They often urged us to move to Maui. We hesitated, because we'd heard from many people that Mother Maui either embraced you or spat you out. But we felt embraced for many years.

At the party the night before the attack, my kitten heels dug into the expansive, manicured lawn overlooking the beach outside of the old Stouffer's Renaissance Hotel in Wailea, a place we'd stayed in the earlier years of our extended visits.

The night was hot and muggy for early May on this part of the island. Some time had passed since we'd seen most of these friends, and they danced by, exuberantly waving and stopping to hug us briefly as the salsa band filled the clear night air. I kicked off my heels and went barefoot in the cool grass.

I wore a strapless, black jersey dress with a hint of spandex. Everything was made with spandex that year. And since I never wore strapless things, I worried about it staying up. And then there was a panty line to worry about. It was too hot to wear underpants or a bra, really. Before we went out, I gave in to removing my underpants and bra, and we danced with abandon on the lush grass. I was wondering when the last time was, if ever, I wore no panties or bra in public. Fortunately, the dress stayed up by itself. But never before in my adult life had I dared do that. It was a first, but I was sixty-three years old and much too late in life to care.

A friend of ours, Jake, and a woman who didn't have to worry about keeping her strapless dress up, sambaed by, both smiling widely, like the winners of *Dancing with the Stars*. His wife stood off alone by the bar, busying herself with a glass of chardonnay.

Our other friends, Fuzzy and Gina, watched from the sidelines, too. Fuzzy wasn't a dancer. Our friend Natalie pulled Wes, her husband, into the circle, until he caught the beat and gyrated around the grass.

Earlier that year, Milo, the architect for the Queen Ka'ahumanu Center, took some time off and rode his bicycle alone down the Pacific Coast Highway from Vancouver to Mexico. Later the night of the party, he told us stories about how logging trucks had tried to run him off the road near Mendocino.

Earlier that evening, Gina told us she had found a strange mole on Fuzzy's arm and was begging Fuzzy to get it checked out.

I looked over at Della and Marvin. They were laughing at a joke that Fuzzy was telling like only he could.

We didn't know it then, but things were changing around us and inside us. Sometimes things changed so insidiously that it all seemed normal. They talked about the increase of drug-related accidents on Haleakala highway by teenagers on crystal meth.

That night, after the party, I slept in the nude. I had only one thin blanket over me. The air was warm and balmy on my skin. Longingly, I wished for a community like this back on the mainland, and wondered if we'd made a mistake by not moving to Maui.

As we slept that night, where was my shark on its long journey to Keawakapu Beach?

A shark can cover hundreds of miles in a day. My shark may have surfed under waves that traveled thousands of miles before it reached the shore of Keawakapu.

Sharks are loners. They swim deep beneath the surface as the wind blows ripples across a calm sea, and those ripples, providing the wind with something to get traction on, build into waves. And as the waves grow in height, the wind pushes them along with increasing force. It speeds them up and builds them higher. It's not the water itself that travels but the wind's energy; in the turbulent medium between air and ocean, water particles move in circles like bicycle pedals that are constantly transferring their energy forward, from swell to crest and back into the trough, then forward again.

My wave, because of the current, could have easily started a week or more before I encountered it. And my shark could have easily been carried along effortlessly during a storm in the warm seas of the South Pacific. Where was it that night we danced? Where was it that night as we slept in our beds at Wailea Ekahi Village?

Was my shark swimming beneath the surface of this energy—darting, indifferent, fierce, looking for prey? Its eyes set back, dark, and chilling. Was it deciding food, not food—live, die? Its teeth set in concentric rows ready to shred, tear, and swallow. Its instinct was to kill and eat. I knew its attack was not personal.

A naturalist at Maui Ocean Center had told us how their fishermen brought baby sharks back in their nets. Employees chose them for their exhibits, and, rather than let them go, the employees hand fed them until they grew too large to be contained in their sealed Plexiglas showcases that tourists roamed past and where the sharks were insulated from their hunt to survive. Finally, once the babies became too large, the employees released them back into the ocean. Do some sharks favor the familiar, salty smell of hands, the fleshy feel of legs and feet because food and humans were connected in their memories? Was my shark one of them?

Was my shark the same one that went on a feeding frenzy and killed the woman, bloodying the waters close to the shore outside of Lahaina while her friend got away, and tourists sat paralyzed and watching in horror from an outdoor seaside restaurant across the street?

Sharks are second only to great white sharks in attacking people. They are consummate scavengers, with excellent senses of sight and smell and a nearly limitless menu of diet items from rubber tires to iron railings. They have sharp, highly serrated teeth, and powerful jaws that can slice through flesh, bone, and turtle shells.

I could imagine being a helpless pray to a shark, and an image came to mind as I dropped off to sleep the night of the party. I remembered spying on my cat as he caught a lizard and ate its good parts in front of me while the lizard's head was left twitching and still alive in the afternoon sun. In my mind's eye, it reminded me of that woman — a helpless prey. But that could never happen to me, just the way I imagined friends getting old dying around me, but I couldn't see dying myself, especially like that woman — in the ocean, eaten by a shark? Come on!

When we arrived on the island a couple of years before, our rental agent was no longer doing business on Maui. We were told by a new rental agent that the former agent's family had suddenly moved off the island back to the mainland when the agent's father hadn't returned from his swim and was assumed drowned after being attacked by a shark. Later we realized that this was the same man whose photo had been on the tree. Although we felt abandoned by our familiar rental agent, we also felt the horror his family must have experienced upon discovering what happened to their father. Was his shark the same one that later attacked me?

A few years before the attack, I had taken on less work in my consulting business and begun painting again. I made my garage into my studio, exhibited my work, and tried to stay ahead of the critic inside my brain by painting to music — quickly, and abstractly. I didn't start with an idea, but let the paint lead me. I seemed to paint mysterious underwater creatures — cerulean blue water, predators erupting out of the sea, and an abstraction of a woman floating in an ocean of shades of transparent blues. When I reflected on this later, it seemed prescient. It was all there, but I didn't see it.

Sharks are powerful and respected animals in Hawaiian lore. It is the tradition in Hawaii that the elderly and the infirmed swim out to meet the shark when they want to pass on to the next world. They call this force the Nā 'Aumakua. At the party the night before my attack, little did I know that I'd be meeting the Hierophant of the Pacific.

6. The Drifters

IT USUALLY TOOK A WHILE for my husband and me to feel comfortable on any vacation: enduring the five-hour airplane ride, searching helplessly to find the lockbox where the rental agent said he put it, struggling with the key to fit it into the front door, opening a creaky lock, and inhaling the first smells of a strange condo that had been closed up for weeks. All the while hoping that an unanticipated disaster would not befall us at least until we got over the jet lag.

I was a difficult traveler. I always ate my way through the flight. I was the passenger who jumped into the air, catching the bags of peanuts like a monkey. From my way of thinking, air travel became a free food zone. I arrived bloated, tired, and disoriented.

No one was in the water when we arrived because it was too murky. I knew that in open ocean swimming, it was important to swim in clear water so I could see where I was going and didn't swim through a school of jellyfish, or face off with a manta or eel. Or worse, in murky water icky, slimy, mysterious things could brush up against me. On the third day, the water cleared. Swimming in the ocean was a different sport than swimming in a pool. I had to stay alert to shifting currents, winds and swells.

I always felt uncomfortable putting on my bathing suit for the first time and assessing my body's change from the previous vacation. It frequently appeared that the food intake was winning the daily battle over the exercise output. I hauled out my snorkel, fins, and goggles, and tried hard not to look and feel like just another tourist when I left our condo. But I always did.

Although Keawakapu Beach was quite empty at eight o'clock in the morning, there were the usual handful of snowbirds taking their morning walk while decked out in their Lands End cruise wear bought especially for this vacation. They'd mysteriously disappear ten days after they came to go back to the snows of Minnesota or Wisconsin. In the breeze of the early morning, not to miss a moment they had paid for, they'd lay their hotel beach towels in the sand and set up their coolers, claiming their spots with colorful umbrellas, ready to camp out for the day. All tourists pretended the beach was theirs, and not to be shared. The names on the hotel towels gave a clue to their sleeping accommodations: Hyatt, Kai Lani, Makena Surf, or Mana Kai — the hotels that dotted the beach.

What caught my eye on this particular morning was the brilliance of the water. Sunlight reflected off the waves like stars rolling on top of white caps. After days of murky sea when we arrived, this day promised to be clear and calm. I anticipated a good, long swim. Swimming had become my religion.

The air smelled of life deep in the sea: sea animals and algae mixing with the shore fragrance of star jasmine growing along the back fences near the dunes.

The sand was warm — not yet hot — from the morning sun, and gritty beneath my toes as I passed a group of men and a few women rolling up their sleeping gear. Several yards away, on the other side of the grassy dunes, mansions rose above hidden paths to the beach that the residents entered through locked gates. I often wondered if the owners feared these drifters who slept on their beach at night.

Drifters were part of the familiar island scenery, as well as the dark underbelly of any resort town. As always, there were a few indigents who lived on the beach or in their cars, which were parked nearby. They kept to the back of the beach, using the rocks and dunes for cover from the sun or rain. In this subtropical climate, it felt safe to assume they were longtime displaced persons. It seemed easy to slip off the grid of the mainland here.

When the clouds rolled in and the chronically flat, robin's-egg blue sky turned dark and threatening, Kihei and upcountry took on the dusty pallor resembling any army town in Arizona or New Mexico. To the tourist's eye, these homeless beach people seemed to become more visible as the lush palms bent in the wind, and rain made the landscape monochromatic.

I'd noticed one drifter in particular many times before, because his unkempt gray hair and blackened teeth frightened me, and because he always smiled at me. I knew that smile. It was left over from the sixties — a blissed out grin. With his long, gray ponytail and tanned, leathery skin, he reminded me of someone who lived in a cave. Strangely, several times I'd seen him playing with three young, blonde-haired children. They couldn't have been more than six years old. Who did they belong to — certainly, not him? I took him to be about sixty years old. What was he doing with small children? On past trips, I'd seen him doing exercises with plastic hand weights in the shallow water. I had purposely gone out of my way to avoid him and not meet his gaze.

That morning, the beach was fairly empty when I ran into the water. I'd learned a technique to quickly put on my fins, goggles, and gloves in waist-high surf facing the waves, so as to not get knocked over by one, and to not waddle like a penguin into the surf in full regalia. In this way, I looked like a pro instead of a tourist. Getting knocked over by a wave was the most embarrassing thing I could imagine doing. I wanted to feel like I was a resident—although I suppose I still fell into the category of tourist even after twenty years of visiting Maui.

7. Panic in the Moment

IN MY PANIC of the moments after the attack, I saw my blood rising to the surface of the water, and where there had been clear water beneath, now there was only a silvery dark mass from end to end. Was I along-side the shark?

I was heading for the shore, hoping to outswim the shark. Realizing that the shark could follow and outswim me, I began swimming slowly and methodically toward the beach while terror roiled in my belly.

Several minutes later, injured and rolling in the swells, helpless and bleeding, while the surf kept pushing me back, I finally got a foothold with my injured leg on the sand at the water's edge. "Help, shark! Help me!" I yelled.

A group of people heard my call, but they walked past me when they saw me in the surf yards to their right. I overheard one say to another, "Tourists who are in the water shouldn't yell like that about sharks. They frighten other tourists."

Shortly after, a couple saw the trail of blood following behind me, and they rushed to help. The man hauled me up to standing and dragged me, hopping on one foot, onto the flat, dry part of the beach. The sand felt gritty and cold. He gently lowered me onto it, tore off his T-shirt, and used it as a tourniquet. I was awash with adrenaline and saw this moment as a pit stop in my marathon to get myself in any way I could to a hospital.

"Call 911!" he shouted. His wife began to punch numbers into her cell phone as I looked at my leg for the first time. Below my knee was a mass of puncture wounds, blood, and shredded skin and flesh. I could see my leg bone, and my foot seemed askew.

It reminded me of the first time I saw a freshly killed goat hanging from a tree in Botswana. I was in the Peace Corps then. The goat was being gutted by the local butcher, whose shop consisted of a tree, a rope, a sharp knife, and lots of horseflies buzzing around the kill. As the butcher carved into the flesh, we all lined up to get our slab of red meat from the goat. I remember that the meat felt still warm to my touch by the time I got back to my hut, made a fire in the open pit, and laid the raw meat above the coals.

The man on the Maui beach who was helping me was a big, beefy white guy in his late fifties. I sat in the sand with both legs spread in front of me.

"I just finished my Community Emergency Response Training in Santa Rosa, California, so I get to practice," he said, obviously trying to keep things light. His wife stood near him, white as a ghost.

"I can't get any phone reception," she said. She was a large breasted woman with a kind face who was about the man's age.

People began to gather around me.

"What happened?" one asked.

That's when I knew I had to stop looking at the blood or I'd go unconscious. I focused on the group of tourists that was now growing around me. Most were young kids and adults. My mind was racing. I felt very intentional. This event must have been entertaining and dramatic to the curiosity-seeking group in the early morning.

"Call my husband. Have you gotten hold of the paramedics?" I shouted. I was filled with adrenaline, but the lower half of my body felt paralyzed.

The man's wife kept trying to reach the paramedics on her cell phone. I'd heard that people bleed to death if they don't get help, or they go into shock, their blood pressure drops dangerously low, and then they die. I peeked at the bleeding wound. I didn't want to black out, so I stayed alert by answering questions from the crowd that seemed to be keep growing—and, like a talk show host, I tried to be entertaining to distract myself when I answered their endless questions:

"Did you see the shark?"

"How big was it?"

"What did it look like?"

"Did it follow you back?"

"How far out were you?"

I talked and talked while the clock in my head kept ticking off how long it was taking for the paramedics to arrive. Where were they? Would I last? And where was my husband?

When I glanced down I saw blood slowly pooling as time wore on. I noticed that I had deep lacerations from my foot going up my calf. Blood puddled and congealed on the surface of the sand, mixing with it. My mind was in a curious place, as if this weren't me. After all, things like this never happened to me. How strange to see the inside of my body—my white bone near the top of my foot, my femur inside my leg—just like the goat hanging from the tree. I was mesmerized, as if looking at a burning building or a train wreck.

Another part of my mind was reflecting, "I wonder how this is going to turn out?" I became calm but focused. It felt strange to be sitting on the beach at this time of day, talking to people who were lookie-loos—curiosity seekers. At the age of sixty-three, it was hard to find people interested in me, an old woman. But I didn't feel old then. I was still a legend in my own mind: a force of nature, an open ocean swimmer, a professional woman, a painter, a writer, a young woman in my own mind. That was my identity. That was who I thought I was and projected this out into the world.

I rewound the tape of the morning in my head. On a normal day, this would have played out differently. I wanted my normal day back. The day was just beginning and I would go back to the condo, have breakfast on the lanai with Ron, and then we'd do something interesting together like we always did, like go to the food and flower market and wander around, then drive upcountry to have dinner with Jake or Wes and Natalie, or maybe Flynn would meet us. It would be like almost every other day on vacation. But I had no willpower to get up and walk away, even if I had been physically able. So, I sat on the sand, waiting for help.

The wife with the cell phone had finally reached my husband. I didn't remember giving her his phone number just a few seconds before, but I must have forgotten in all the confusion.

"Your wife is here on the public beach. She was just attacked by a shark. Come down to the beach below the public parking now." She sounded demanding, as if irritated at trying to get her words through. After all, she didn't know this stranger. She wanted to impress the severity of the situation on him.

"He sounded groggy. I think I woke him up," she said as she hung up the phone. I could imagine him just waking up—not a good time of day for him—and getting this phone call.

"We're celebrating our twenty-second wedding anniversary this summer," I said to her by way of conversation, but inside I was trying to normalize this bizarre situation somehow.

Also, I was trying to hold off the fear that was growing in my belly as I came to realize that I was in the middle of something awful, and that I no longer had magical powers of permanence. I could not will this away!

Suddenly, the homeless man I had seen earlier was walking toward me in the sand. He didn't greet me with words, just a nod and that enigmatic smile on his face. The crowd parted tentatively, and he sat down behind me, straddling me like a couch cushion. It must have appeared to the crowd that had formed that he somehow knew me, but he didn't. Without asking, he put his hand in the middle of my back, opposite my heart, and whispered, "Keep breathing." My body lurched and then leaned into his. I gave a deep long breath and relaxed for the first time since I had tumbled onto the shore.

Up to that point, I'd been in my kick-ass survival mind. I'd been schooled in being able to think my way through anything—or so I thought. Accidents, illness, and death happened to other people, not me.

"Did you call 911?" I asked the man's wife. "Why are they taking so long?"

"They are on their way," she reassured me.

Why did I suddenly trust this homeless man whom I had previously been wary of? Perhaps because this man reassured me silently in a way that I didn't know I needed. He was speaking to my heart. He was reminding me to breathe, the way a rabbi or priest would.

I surrendered into the help that he offered. He tapped into the indescribable and ineffable mystery that I had been unknowingly longing for. He knew my terror, and not in the fix-it way that most people used to ward off their own fear. I surrendered into the palm of his hand on my back and the weight of his strong body. I lay there feeling perfectly comfortable, leaning into him in silence, while another part of me felt awkward. How was I going to reconcile this with myself later? It was a silly thought, and an uncomfortable one.

Finally, I saw the paramedics in the distance, lurching towards me, their feet dragging in the sand like they were bogged down in a snowdrift. Their stubborn equipment was not made for sandy beaches: a steel gurney and a huge fire hose. Each of the three men looked like they had just come off a bender from the night before—bedraggled, in swimsuits and dirty T-shirts. The sight was not a real confidence builder. They dragged the hose out to its full length, aimed it, then yelled at another guy who was a quarter of a mile back near the fire truck, "Let her rip!" and rip she did. The water filled the length of the hose and then it spurted out and headed straight towards my leg and foot.

"No! You can't use that on me," I cried out. I pictured the force used on buildings and roofs; I pictured it blowing off my leg.

"We got to, lady. We have orders to irrigate the wound before we bring you to the hospital so that no infection sets in and we have to amputate." They turned the pressure of the fire hose up.

Within seconds and without hesitation, the full blast of the high-pressure hose, like the one police use on rioters, let loose on my leg. I stepped off into oblivion with pain, and lost the part of me called my mind. Everything went black.

8. Paramedics on the Beach

LATER I REMEMBERED the paramedics carrying me, half conscious on a vinyl stretcher, back across the hot sand to the waiting ambulance in the public parking lot with the siren blaring over the pounding waves. When they transferred me to a gurney and pushed it onto the back of the ambulance, it bumped against the fender, made a metal against metal crashing sound, and startled me to full alertness. It was then that I saw familiar faces in the crowd — recognizable faces — that had followed us from the beach. There was my husband, Ron, in his sweatpants under his bathrobe, and that toothless man standing side-by-side about two yards from the open back doors of the ambulance. They couldn't have been more different in appearances: Ron, tall, broad shouldered, blue eyed and a full head of silver hair next to a man a little taller than me who was looking up at him. They were talking together. I remember waving to them: the kind of wave with elbow bent and open hand that Queen Elizabeth gave to crowds. A small silliness at my gesture washed over me. It was the kind of gesture that was a code to my husband that I was okay. The kind of private humor between partners. Things were beginning to move now. I wanted everyone to hurry up, and I felt relieved I'd finally get to the hospital before I bled out or worse.

My husband face looked ashen. The phone call must have just woken him. I sat up on the gurney to see him more clearly. He looked gaunt, exhausted, and puzzled at all this commotion surrounding the ambulance. Then the doors slammed shut.

Inside the van, it was just me and a young paramedic in a very small space covered by a low roof. The walls were crowded with all kinds of devices and hoses. The guy had to squat next to me to help me. His hand shook as he tried to find my vein. I noted that he looked worse than I felt. I wondered if he had partied too much the night before, so I helped him find a big vein. For God's sake, I thought. Do I have to do the triage, too?

"Lie down for the ride," he said.

"I can't, because I'll get carsick."

"It's a forty-five-minute ride at this hour," he said.

He moved the gurney to a more upright position. Occasionally, I'd open my eyes. He looked gray, and his hands were still shaking. Had he never seen a shark bite, or was it the thought of a shark attack that frightened him so much? The ambulance was moving through traffic on Pukalani Highway.

We rode in silence. I'd never been in an ambulance before, and now my leg was aching. He raised it, using a hard pillow. My mind was willing the ambulance to go faster as it wove in and out of traffic, taking the upper road to Maui Memorial Hospital. Out of the windows of the back doors, I could see cars stopped on the shoulder to let the ambulance through. My life had taken a new turn, and I was observing it with a kind of onlooker's curiosity, wondering why cars behind us had pulled over, forgetting that I was in the ambulance. My mind was slipping, and beneath the surface I was willing my way back to the condo after perhaps a Band-Aid and a few stitches. I'd go home the same day. That evening, friends would come by and, over a glass of wine, I'd tell them about my adventure with the shark that morning. At the same time, another part of me was feeling a dread I'd only rarely known.

What a stupid little god I'd been, believing that I was invincible and enjoying a personal relationship with the divine. At the same time, out of nowhere, this moment in the ambulance was suddenly mixed with anxiety and excitement. We were all on this one mission to get to Maui Memorial Hospital. Meanwhile, in the back of my mind, I remembered friends telling me that the hospital had a terrible track record of mortality and patient infection. This island was a destination resort, not a place where you could afford to get sick.

The paramedic was rendering saline solution, and taking my blood pressure and pulse. Cars honked, parted, and the siren blared. At first I didn't understand that it was blaring from our ambulance, with me inside. I was quickly losing my sense of time and space.

Mother Maui either embraces you or spits you out, our friends had told us. Was Mother Maui spitting me out? What else was spitting me out?

My mind went back to a time when we used to skip pebbles over the water. One thing reminded me of another thing, and then it would skip farther out to yet another thing, like the pebbles we threw.

The summer was 1954. I was afraid of the water and the waves at Bradley Beach. What a vast expanse of uncertainty lapped up my legs and against my bony body.

I was ten years old in a black and white photo that I still have tucked away in an album. Mom took a deckled edged picture with her brownie camera. I had on a new, blue-print bathing suit with a little blue-print, ruffled skirt.

My face was a smiling mask squinting into the sun. I can still remember how I felt that day. The Atlantic surf crashed behind me in a cloudless New Jersey sky.

My mother knew that I was afraid of the water, and she had been holding me afloat in the shallows as the waves crashed behind us and pushed us closer and closer to shore, so we'd have to keep moving back out into the deeper part of the ocean.

My mother was an excellent swimmer, and once she got it in her head that I was going to learn something, she could make anything happen by force of her will.

"Mom! Look! We're drifting out to sea. Let me go. I wanna go back," I yelled over the crashing waves.

"Just let me show your dad that you can swim! We'll move closer to shore." She pushed me from the back into the shore and yelled to my dad, who was standing nearby.

"Look, Bernie! Our daughter can swim," my mom said.

I stood in the water. My flowered bathing suit felt sticky on my sun-dried skin. My hair tasted salty, and stuck to my scalp as I squinted into the camera. My fake smile was a demonstration of strength and confidence to win my parents' approval.

I watched my father leap over the swells on the sandy shore that afternoon. He looked like he was headed straight out to Europe. Well, for the first couple of hundred yards. Then he stopped behind a big wave, disappeared, and swam back to shore with his head above water, his arms windmilling about him and dragging the rest of his body behind him.

He smelled like fish when he stumbled onto the hot sand, his suit clinging to his robust belly. He looked like a beached whale.

"You can swim," he said, grabbing my arm. I pulled away. He gave me a weak whack on my seat. My wet bathing suit bottom absorbed the smack.

I stood on the edge of the shore. Hundreds of mothers, fathers, grandparents, and kids were yelling, running, screaming, and flying recklessly into the surf. My stomach churned with each wave that crashed at my feet. That summer day I vowed to never go into the ocean again. Swimming was yet another thing I didn't feel safe doing.

Years later, just weeks before graduation from college, word came from the dean's office that seniors couldn't graduate unless they demonstrated that they could swim the length of the pool. All seniors had to meet this water safety requirement in order to get their degree. I had never even seen the pool, much less set foot in it, during the four years I'd been in college. I was blindsided.

There were girls in that college who'd come from Miss Parson's Bay Mountain Prep, or Maplewood Day School, who'd played tennis in their diapers, worn A-line tennis skirts, and ridden horses all their lives. They could effortlessly swim the English Channel if asked.

Then there was me. "Exercise could kill you," my dad had said as I was growing up, but Mom, being a nurse, encouraged me. She wanted me to be an excellent swimmer just like she had been when she was growing up.

When we saw people playing tennis in the park, my father would say, People ought to read books, study, or learn how to play the violin. Look at Albert Einstein. He invented something. These people knock themselves out for what?" My mother would roll her eyes at him for his myopic observations. After all, she was a nurse, and she knew what was good for people.

So in the spring of my senior year, after class, I hauled myself down to the college pool, slipped into the shallow end, fear clutching my insides. So much was at stake. How could I go home and tell my parents that I hadn't graduated college because I couldn't swim?

I strained my arms and legs to reach the twenty-five-meter finish. I realized two things: one, I had to rely on myself, because no one was going to come to my rescue, and two, that I could drown. I had to learn how to be comfortable in the water. I had to learn how to swim well.

Now as I lay in the emergency area hallway in the hospital waiting to be seen, I felt a wildness inside me. Anxious thoughts arose from unsettling memories. All those years growing up and never being encouraged to feel my body in a way that didn't bring shame and disregard for myself. It was only long after those years, when I had put many miles of distance between my family and myself, that I began to explore the mysteries of my body — and water was the medium: buoyant, light, and transparent. All my muscles and bones responded to it in a way that I'd never experienced before. It was only after many years and many water experiences that I felt fully comfortable in the water.

Suddenly, time speeded up. I was laying on a gurney in the hallway of the emergency room in my damp bathing suit, when a doctor appeared. She wasn't talking to me — she was on her cell phone with another person, and from the conversation, I assumed it was another doctor.

"I need your help. We've stopped the bleeding, but I need you to look at her leg and decide if we must amputate it or not."

She glanced over at me and saw that my eyes were open. She moved a few steps away to continue her conversation, but I could still hear her.

"I've never done a shark bite. Yes, it was a shark. I'm a general surgeon, you are orthopedic—a specialist. I don't care about how good the surf is today. Get your ass down here—we need you now."

Then Ron, Wes, and Jake were standing in a huddle beside her in the narrow hallway. They seemed to be listening and talking all at the same time.

"Yes, I've called in another doctor to perform the surgery. He's a specialist that just arrived on the island with his wife from Massachusetts," the general surgeon said.

"Massachusetts" put my rattled mind at ease momentarily. The state had credibility. Pilgrims. Stoic, strong, and enduring people.

"We might have to amputate, but we won't know until we get in there and see the damage—he's an orthopedic surgeon. He'll perform the operation within the next few hours."

Then there was some back and forth: Ron's voice, the doctor's voice, Wes's voice. I closed my eyes. When I opened them, they were all gone.

The emergency hallway was silent—maybe a lull between peak times—but every now and then I heard an electronic sound. Had I been dreaming? At the top of the list was amputation? Would I be taking an unexpected turn in my life? Never feeling whole in this lifetime? Never again feeling those petty but superior feelings of a life of luck and ascent—an ordinary beginning to becoming a success. Someone who didn't have to ask for help.

What if I died? Didn't people die every year in the operating rooms in the United States? Didn't I read that James Brown's wife died when she didn't wake up from the anesthesia? My mother, a hospital nurse, told me when I was a small. girl that most people die alone. They don't want others to worry about them, so they "are taken" during the early hours of the morning, with no one to turn to. I had to rely on myself out at sea. It felt good to be so alone and dependent on no one, and it also felt scary—the fascination of always testing myself—but I didn't feel that way here in the hospital.

In my life on land, there was the surprising kindness of a stranger, or a lucky break. There in the wilderness of the ocean, there was an impersonality I'd experienced in nature: birth, growth, and death. The never-ending cycle of life.

How was that supposed to inform my beliefs about faith or religion? Was it ashes to ashes? Was it a mysterious God? Was I being punished for something I was too stupid to figure out?

I was feeling a chill from being in the corridor of the emergency room, waiting. I was too tired to ask what was happening. Was another doctor going to arrive? Was a room upstairs in the hospital being readied? My thoughts shoved me into catastrophizing, rewriting the episode: I saw myself swimming alone when a shark came up behind me. In one gesture, he separated my body and my torso. My mind kept planning, working, thinking, but my torso floated away. I looked down and saw that my leg was gone. I'd lost my leg. It was floating away in the salty ocean farther and farther from help. My dad was beside me. I couldn't swim. He kept yelling, "Swim, swim!"

I began to scream. Would I see a stump where my leg used to be when I woke up? I'd only seen this in old sailor movies. Do they tell you first? Don't they prepare you for the shock?

9. Emergency Room

I DON'T KNOW HOW LONG I waited in the corridor of the ER. Finally, I felt some movement on the gurney. The clicking gurney wheels moved in a scurry-scurry, dawdle fashion—stop, start, stop, start. Two attendants wheeled me into a big elevator, then the door softly closed. In a few moments, I was wheeled into a high-ceilinged, large, cold room with lots of machines softly buzzing. A male doctor introduced himself as my anesthesiologist, and I remembered the word "Massachusetts" and felt safe. I wasn't thinking clearly or I would have known he wasn't the orthopedic surgeon from New England. The anesthesiologist quickly and adroitly found a vein, then carefully inserted a needle into my arm. I was going unconscious when I realized he wasn't the same doctor I'd heard about in the hallway.

I awoke. Startled. It all came back: The shark, the beach, the ambulance, waiting in the hallway outside the emergency room for surgery, the seconds before being put under, then sleep.

I was in a hospital room. My first thought was: did I still have my leg? There it was, still attached. A huge white bandage, stiff and slightly smelling of a chemical I associated with cleanliness cradled my leg like a swaddle for a newborn baby.

Why would I still have my leg if they said they might have to amputate? Maybe not right now, but later—another operation? My momentary relief turned to worry.

The hospital room was still. Outside in the corridor the sounds of health commerce still went on—humming respirators, gurney wheels clicking along the linoleum floor, layers of murmurings from other rooms.

I wiggled my toes and peeked inside. My toes were still there. Within the thick bandage, my leg was trussed like a thanksgiving turkey sown closed with stuffing. I felt a familiar tingling up my leg. It was then that I knew each one of my toes, criticized in the past for being short, stubby, and not easily articulated in yoga class, my heel, my ankles, my calf and my thighs, which I had loathed all my life—everything was still there for now, and felt like it was in place.

They say that certain Eastern European Jews — Ashkenazi, and I belong to that tribe — are prone to depression. It's part of our DNA, but on this day, at that moment, I was giddy with life. I was elated! Truly elated. I was alive!

Light filled the room in a rosy haze. The sheets smelled clean and crisp. I touched my new addition of a thickly wrapped bandage I'd come through. Something opened in my brow, and my mind felt clear, lifting off like a helium balloon. I was no longer the same person I had been before eight o'clock in the morning the day before.

For the past year, I had been locked into the routine of caregiving for Ron, after his open-heart surgery. I learned that if patients don't have someone by their side advocating for them, sensitive and vigilant, good hospital care is hard to get during recovery. What was constantly present during that time was a sadness so palpable that often I couldn't speak of it. The healing process can become burdensome for the caregiver, too. During that previous year, he had survived and recovered slowly while I had sat by his bedside at home many an afternoon, wondering where the undertow of my life was taking me. I was losing myself.

After the open-heart surgery, while Ron was healing, one afternoon as the sun cast a long golden shadow across his hospital bed, a friend named Marvin came to visit and insisted on viewing the seven-inch gash down Ron's chest. I couldn't look, so I busied myself paying bills and calling the water company to let them know the check would be late and explaining why. The distraction of this purposeful behavior momentarily soothed me. I only looked back when I heard Della, Marvin's wife, sing Ron a poem she had written.

Little did we know that things were changing slowly on the island in and around us. The following year, Della contracted cervical cancer and was dead within eleven months. She refused conventional treatment and died in her garden.

Now, in my own hospital bed, I reminded myself that I had another purpose. I had pulled something precious from a deep, dark pit. I had reclaimed myself in this act of saving myself. I had not gone over an emotional cliff. I had not panicked. I had beaten the odds — for now, at least.

At that moment, a nurse came in and the silence erupted into a brusque voice.

"I'll shut off the morphine now."

She grabbed the plastic line that was buried under the covers.

"My God! You never touched the morphine all night," she said.

"I thought it dripped in by itself, like in the television progr confused by the half-dozen plastic bags hanging above my he through small transparent tubes into my arm.

"No, honey. This is a self-administering button. This is hospital. You've got to push the button every ten minutes to get the mor into your system. Didn't anyone tell you that?" She found the button buried under the pillows and pulled it out.

Just as I was about to respond, a boyish-looking man who couldn't have been more than thirty-five entered, dressed in olive-colored scrubs, a loose V-neck top, and pants held up with a drawstring tied to his slim hips. He had a strong jaw and startlingly green eyes. He strode across the room to my bedside, his wooden shoes making a clopping sound that heightened his tall build with an air of authority.

I was in the middle of shouting, so elated was I with my new life, "Don't let it go to waste! Let me try some morphine now. I have health insurance!"

"You've lost your chance," he told me with a smile, grabbed the line, handed it to the nurse, and introduced himself as Dr. Toma.

"You look like Doogie Howser," I told him.

"You're either delirious, or overmedicated; I pumped enough drugs into your leg and foot during surgery to kill a shark." He laughed.

I laughed, too.

I felt momentarily reassured that there was a doctor in the house, and I had someone to blame if anything went wrong. I didn't know what had gotten into me. I didn't know this man. I had never talked to a doctor in such a casual way, but he seemed to have an intimate knowledge of me, which he confirmed.

"I've already spent four hours operating on your leg, so I feel like we are old friends." He paused. "You are not out of the woods yet," he said. "We have to wait and see." Despite my euphoria, I was too drugged to respond.

The nurse slipped out with the morphine kit, and there I lay in a strangely contoured position in the hospital bed.

With the doctor still there, I took a look around, because this was the first time I'd had a chance to look at my surroundings. A vast white room opened around me. It was vacant except for a two-tier empty bookcase on my right, one chair, and many bags of liquid that hung from separate hooks on a metal contraption that looked like a coat rack on wheels. It was positioned next to my bed.

The room was relentlessly white. When I looked out the open door to my room, I saw a corridor that ended at a wall with a window, so I knew I was in last room at the far end of a long, wide hallway. My bed on wheels looked like someone had just dropped the bed off because it sat diagonally in the middle of the linoleum floor. And one wall seemed to have a large picture window behind a closed, heavily-draped curtain.

If I moved, the contraption of bags moved with me. I sensed that with large movements, the tape and needles would pull on the bags attached to long, clear tubes, and would hurt terribly.

"You have to stay here for five days because we're not sure you won't get septicemia or some infection where we'd still have to amputate. You might get a drop foot even if this operation proves successful. We won't know for a while. You're still in the weeds," said Dr. Toma. My elation quickly turned to claustrophobia.

"How many shark bites have you done?" I asked.

"None, actually. I've never done surgery on a shark bite before, but I worked on an eel bite once."

He tugged at his olive-colored, square-shaped cap, gave me a big smile, and left.

Dr. Toma's credibility spiraled downward.

A nurse walked across the room and pulled open the drapes. Brilliant sunlight flooded the room with a dead-on view of Haleakala—the sleeping volcano that last erupted in 1801 and spewed molten lava and ash down the southwestern side of Maui. Outside the window were lush green hills, palm trees, and the verdant volcano. The vortex of the white room spread all around me. I felt disoriented—a feeling that was such a curious contrast to the ocean with all its depths to explore, and where I could really feel myself in my body. In here, there was only silence in a hospital room at the end of a corridor.

Haleakala was the five-star attraction of the island. Tourists arrived at the top of the volcano by all means of transportation. They bicycled up, starting at five in the morning just before the sun reached the horizon; they helicoptered in, or they hiked in. Here I was—such irony, with a front row seat.

After he had recovered from a long bout with cancer while spending eight months in the city hospital, a friend told me that he could tell whether he was in good or bad shape by the view outside his hospital window. When his view looked out onto the air conditioning system of the building, he knew he was recovering. However, when he had a view of the distant Golden Gate Bridge, he knew he was in trouble. Judging from the view out my window, my prognosis didn't look good.

Alone now, memories of my encounters with eels demanded attention: open ocean swimming with eels shooting out from behind dead coral, with their pointy faces and darting eyes. They were more afraid of me than I was of them. Dr. Doogie Howser's only experience was doing surgery on an eel bite? He was comparing an eel bite to my shark bite? Wasn't that like comparing the size and strength of a house cat to a mountain lion? I was beginning to feel a dull ache throbbing down my right leg, and in my right foot. My confidence in his handiwork was waning.

Night fell. This end of the hospital was very quiet — still, in fact, and I began to contemplate about the quality of the stillness. The stillness felt like a classical symphony filling my ears with soothing and refreshing music. I imagined that Ron was back at the condo, and I felt relieved that he was nearby. A strange relief, because he was really about forty-five minutes away, but because we were on an island, he felt closer somehow.

Who was this person called "me," anyway? My thoughts were in flux inside. My mind felt slowed down and restless. Already I had napped and gazed at the volcano outside my window. Five days of waiting for a decision about my leg seemed endless to me lying in bed. What was I supposed to do with myself? I couldn't imagine staring at the volcano all by myself indefinitely for the remainder of my time in the hospital.

I used to tease my girlfriend, who had retired after thirty years of elementary school teaching but continued to keep a busy retirement schedule and was constantly on the go. I had to schedule lunches with her two weeks in advance to get on her "dance card." Was I like that, swimming four miles a day and finding a myriad of things to do even while on vacation? Filling my suitcase with books and projects to take with me?

The crisis of the last twenty-four hours filtered through my mind. I drifted off to sleep, fighting back the dark thunderheads of a possible amputation.

10. The Reporters

AROUND SEVEN O'CLOCK the next morning, I was awakened by a robust, blonde woman wearing a red sports jacket, pantyhose, and heels and looking like she had stepped right out of the Financial District of San Francisco — out of place in this humid climate.

"I hope you're feeling better," she gushed. "I'm Susan Strong, the public relations spokesperson for Maui Memorial Community Hospital. How are you doing?"

"I'm okay."

"We have some reporters waiting in the lobby to talk to you about the shark attack."

"What? Why are so many people interested in this?"

"Well, this is a big deal." She looked much younger than me, and she emphasized "big deal," elongating the two words, and at the end of each sentence her voice rose into a question. "When someone gets attacked by a shark, everyone gets interested. I'd say it's the 'Jaws Thing.' People fear sharks, and even want them all killed around here. There's curiosity, since you had a brush with death."

"But Jaws — well, that was in the Atlantic Ocean." I had never thought for a moment about me being eaten by a shark in all the years I swam in the Pacific Ocean. It only happened to others, as in other people who die — never me."

"We even have the Honolulu Advertiser and other reporters downstairs. How they got wind of you, I'll never know." She elongated the words "never know." "I was hoping you'd talk to them. Tell them what good care you are receiving. Lately, we've been getting such poor publicity about our hospital." She paused and added with awe, "Even Associated Press reporters are waiting." Again, she ended the sentence with a question mark.

At that moment, my husband walked in. Susan Strong introduced herself to him.

"What's going on?" he asked her.

"Well, we want some reporters to interview her," she said, pointing to my leg. She pulled out yesterday's paper and showed it to him while I looked on. Ron read it aloud to me.

Maui News Kihei, Maui May 7, 2007

A man on a stand-up paddleboard reported he had been stalked by an 18-foot tiger shark while paddling several hundred yards offshore about 7:30 a.m. The man told county ocean safety officers the shark followed him along-side his boat for a good distance before the man decided to head in to the beach at Kameole Beach Park, less than 2 miles north of Keawakapu.

The shark attack that occurred off of Keawakapu Beach in Kihei was reported at 8:34 a.m. by a bystander on the beach. The victim, a 63-year-old woman swimmer, was taken to Maui Memorial Hospital by ambulance."

He handed the folded paper back to her.

"She just got out of surgery and she's still recovering. She's in no shape to talk to reporters," Ron said.

The woman said to my husband, "But we *even* have the Associated Press downstairs."

"Look, I'm recovering from open heart surgery. I can't take any more stress — nor can she."

"I'm fine," I told them. "I want to do this. I don't want to be holed up in this bed in this hospital staring out the window for five days."

He turned towards me. "You don't mind if I'm not here when you talk to them? I'm trying to find us another condo that you can return to without the construction noise next door. You can do this without me."

"Fine," I said firmly. Actually, I was relieved to be handling this my way.

Then he turned back to Susan Strong.

"We rented a condo not knowing that it was right next to one that was being remodeled. We decided to come to Maui because our neighbors in Mill Valley were in the middle of construction — and the noise. And now this! We awake to the chaos that starts at seven in the morning and ends at eight at night. It's so noisy that you can't even think — jackhammers and drills all day, way into the evening. This is not what we signed up for on our vacation."

"Oh, I didn't know. You guys have been through a lot — I understand."

As they talked, I saw myself lying alone staring at the walls all day long. Life gets funny when you have too much time on your hands to think. What flashed across my mental screen at that moment was something Anne Lamott often said, "My mind is a bad neighborhood. I don't like to go in there by myself."

"Yes, I want to do this," I told them again. "I feel okay." I wasn't in pain at that moment.

As the sun was rising in the sky over the volcano, two nurses helped me up. I felt shaky planting my left foot on the floor for the first time since the operation, making a little hop and turn, and landing in the wheelchair. Then they wheeled me downstairs to a large conference room. Susan Strong stood beside me, holding a banner that announced in large block letters: *Maui Memorial Hospital: Where Community Serves Its People.* About forty reporters shuffled into the room. At first, they were tentative and quiet, standing far back by the door. One reporter broke the silence by asking how I felt.

"I'm feeling okay." I smiled, wondering why they were hanging back. I'd seen paparazzi running aggressively after people. These reporters seemed afraid of me. I was so glad to be alive that I wanted to talk to everyone. I beckoned them closer.

Suddenly Susan Strong beamed from ear to ear and moved close to my wheelchair, my bandaged leg thrust out before me.

"What was it like?" An older reporter threw out the first question.

"I think the shark came up behind me, because I didn't see him. I'm glad I'm in one piece."

The reporters as a group moved even closer. I seemed to hear a collective sigh. Clicks from cameras went off with flashes of lights.

I'd been interviewed by the press before because I'd written four books and had given many speeches in front of larger audiences all over the country, but this situation was new—forty men of all ages with cameras, lights, and recorders surrounded me.

"Did you know that the shark had been seen from a beach a mile and a half away about an hour before?"

"If I'd known, I wouldn't have gone in the water. I wasn't warned,"

"Weren't you afraid of one of the deadliest creatures in the sea? They say that tiger sharks are the largest predator on the food chain, next to great white."

"Well, I didn't hear the *Jaws* music. I only heard my heart pounding. First I thought the creature in the water was a large sea turtle, but my new swim fin popped off, and it went flying over the swells. Then I saw a wall of gray, and realized it was a shark."

"Aren't you afraid to swim in the ocean at your age?" a younger reporter inquired.

"My age? What do you mean? Can't a sixty-three-year-old woman swim in the ocean? Is there an age limit?" I snapped back.

There was a moment of hushed embarrassment, and then the young reporter spoke.

"I didn't mean that. I just meant that most people swim in pairs."

"I don't like to keep pace with other swimmers. I like to stop and look at things whenever I want."

"Do you want the Coast Guard to go out and kill the shark?"

"No. This is sea life. It's nature. I was in its territory. I'm just surprised it was me who was attacked. I want my fin back. I'm just grateful that I have all my body parts."

"The last shark attack occurred last year—about six months ago—in the same area. It was one of four Hawaii shark attacks in 2006," recounted a reporter.

"We've had several people die from these attacks," said another. "You were very lucky."

"I didn't know that because those attacks must have been downplayed; no one ever talks about them. If it weren't for some kind people, I wouldn't be here now. I want to thank the people who rescued me from the water. I could have bled out, but one man put a torn T-shirt on my leg for a tourniquet. His wife called the paramedics and my husband. She had a cell phone with her. Another let me lean against him and reminded me to breathe until the paramedics came."

How do you describe a brush with death while trying to keep it together, be articulate, and appear calm to strangers? Inside, I was falling apart. I felt like I had to be entertaining and upbeat—like I'd done most of my life to get people's attention. Maybe this was too much for me after all. Maybe Ron had been right; I could feel my energy taking a downward turn, and I could feel the drugs wearing off. Maybe the elation was the drug high from all the anesthesia, as well as the drugs used to numb the pain in my leg. I needed to lie down before this act of courage deteriorated into a bad joke.

Susan Strong saw that I was fading,

"I can see our patient is relieved to have this behind her, and now it's best to get her back to her room for rest," she announced.

She politely ended the interview, took hold of the wheelchair, and slowly guided me out into the corridor, into the elevator, to the room, and back into bed. I could tell she was happy about the meeting because she couldn't stop talking.

"You did that so well — you'd think you were a pro at this. You were funny, too. Reporters like sound-bytes like you gave."

Don't you just love people that make such undervaluing statements about who you are and what you are capable of sometimes? I thought. I was getting cranky.

The pain was rising in my leg and moving upwards. After Susan Strong left, I felt my joy ebbing away. I was beginning to again feel that this was not a sprint but a marathon. I closed my eyes for a moment and then opened them, not knowing where I was. I wondered if I'd ever find my way back home to the condo in Wailea, or even Marin.

I lay on my back, staring at the ceiling as a nurse reconnected me to the tubes and inserted a new medication into a port. Soon, my thoughts were spinning, and in my memory what came into sharp focus was our home in Mill Valley. Would I ever get back home again? How would I deal with an amputated leg? It was a thought I couldn't deal with at the moment.

When was the last time I was ill and had to lie in bed? When did I even think about the distance I've come in sixty-three years? The comment about my age annoyed me, and I wondered exactly what annoyed me about it. Was it because I noticed that those reporters were not seeing me as an able-bodied, attractive woman? The way I saw myself. They saw me as an over-the-hill matron. I was an old lady to them. I'd had a moment like that before. It was when I was standing at the side of my father's bed when he breathed his last breath. I'd experienced an almost physical push from behind and clearly felt a sense that I had moved up in the queue of mortality.

You look at your watch one minute and it's only eight thirty at night — the night is young, and you've got all the time in the world. And then suddenly and without warning, it's ten o'clock and you have to leave the celebration because you have to go to work the next day. It's like taking a nap in the middle of the afternoon, and then waking up to darkness outside. You don't know what day it is, or what time it is. I was appalled by all the time I had lost. I didn't feel old. I felt younger than most other people my age. Yes, I was sixty-three, but I never considered myself to really be that old. I wasn't infirm. I never got colds or the flu. I had breast cancer in 1990, but I don't remember being there emotionally to experience it. I had been paralyzed with fear during and after the diagnosis, surgery, and recovery. In a way, I felt like I'd played hooky from life. Why didn't I spend my life doing more adventurous things? Such as staying in Africa with gorillas, maybe, like Jane Goodall, or interviewing combat soldiers in Iraq, like Christian Amanpour? I guess if you blow through your life for as long as you want, you still have to pay the piper.

Growing up, I had always wanted to be an artist, but my mother said that artists starve. Teachers can always get a job. I could only go to college if I studied to be a teacher at a "real" college, not a technical school. My mother's dream for me was to marry a doctor and become a teacher with a secure job (in case anything happened to my husband). Every Jewish mother's dream.

I fulfilled part of her dream by the time I was thirty, but as far as the doctor part, I became a doctor myself. It was a doctorate of psychology, but I was a doctor, after all. Then I went on to build my own consulting business that successfully competed with the big boy firms in the Bay Area. Twenty years after I divorced my college sweetheart, I married my Ron. My mom abandoned her unfulfilled hopes of having grandchildren, and my dad breathed an audible sigh of relief that I was marrying again. "Now someone else can feel responsible for my little girl," he said. I guess they were normal Jewish parents in that respect. At the age of fifty-five, I went back to painting and entering art shows. The underwater world had seeped into my paintings and my psyche.

Lying in the hospital bed, I was wandering in this wilderness of my mind. But this was not a forest of trees and sun dappled leaves, paths, deer, and soft breezes. This was a wilderness I was remembering of vastness, hot sun, cold waters, and horizon as far as my eyes could see. I'd never felt my body this way before: slick, sleek, moving limb by limb, strong, and coordinated. Was the shark inside me now? Was I seeing through his eyes? Did the shark give me a Shakti transmission — energy from a powerful source? Would I know? Or would I find out much later? I'd heard of transmissions from gurus, but what about an eighteen-foot, three-thousand-pound shark guru? A guru who knew the depths of the oceans, and was the lethal queen of the seas? The ocean is a vast wildness of all kinds of life — from stinging jellyfish, mantas, and eels, to ominous creatures.

In my mind, I retraced the route I took each morning from Keawakapu Beach to Ulua Beach and back. The route I swam was in the trough made by waves that broke against the breakers that jutted out past the waves. We used to call them jetties on the East Coast. Some mornings, I swam past thousands of iridescent fish the size of sardines, seemingly asleep in a gelatinous web that bound them together as the ocean swayed them in the continuous current that went back and forth. A couple of times I came very close to two six-foot manta rays feeding on the underside of a catamaran that was anchored off shore. The eels darted out from coral at forty foot depths, and the puffer fish reminded me of people I knew: they swam in circles, keeping tight control over their territory. My favorites were the Moorish idols, yellow and black—or the Christmas Wrasses with red-and-green markings.

This underwater wilderness was treacherous and wild. It was not a swimming pool. I had to be alert to changing currents, tides, and weather, but I was also driven by my curiosity about the watery world around me. On land, with concrete or dirt most often beneath me, it was second nature to be alert to danger: a dark alleyway, a busy intersection, or a crowd of people watching a street mime as I remembered to clutch my purse—but here in the depths of forty feet, the ocean had a new and second language. And I chose to swim it alone.

I came to dislike the swim groups like the hospitality of Fork and Float, or snorkeling with others who swam at differing paces with differing levels of curiosity: The Sierra Club of the Seas. It took all the fun out of the ocean for me. It was like following and keeping up with a herd of sheep. I preferred enjoying my own company. There was something about being alone in the ocean that made me feel androgynous. I was eyes and ears and an ageless, agile body.

In the watery wilderness, there was an impersonality. Nothing was without its enemies and nothing was without its dangers, but the beauty was seductive, and frequently the idea of just turning right and heading to Japan did cross my mind. What was a little bit farther out? Would I be able to get back? There was always the thought that I needed to reserve enough energy to return. I could get muddled and lose my sense of direction. I had no one to turn to except myself.

As I dozed, "Mr. Tambourine Man" filtered down the hospital corridor and drifted into my room. With my eyes closed, I mouthed the words that came back to me, and I felt that old longing for my youth when I felt like I had some mysterious future.

Slowly, feelings faded into the cotton wool of my mind as I drifted into a fitful sleep wondering about amputation.

.

11. Remembering Unsafe Places

I WOKE EARLY. Whoever said you can get rest in the hospital was wrong.

The nurse had just finished changing the lactate ringer bag hanging from the device on the left side of my bed when my husband walked in.

"I just came by to see the shark girl," Ron said. Under his arm, he had a paper bag. He held it over the bed.

"Is it chocolate?"

"No. It's a fin? I found it on the beach this morning. I guess this was the one that the shark spat up after it spat you out! There's a shark swimming around out there with a black and blue nose, thanks to you."

He handed me a well-worn rubber fin.

"Hey, let's make the bookcase an altar!" he said. "We can put the fin up there so you can meditate on it while you recover." He walked across the room and put the worn fin on the top bookcase shelf. Then walked out the door, and returned with a chair with arms that he placed nearer my bed.

"Did you know that you've made every paper on the island and on the mainland? Last night I got back to the condo to relax, and I saw you on every news channel. Oh, by the way, your brother called. I guess he saw the story in a paper on the East Coast. Associated Press carried the story. He left a voice message and there was a kahuna in the lobby that I met who wants to meet you. He said this was an important initiation for you."

"An initiation?"

"Yes—like a test to move you to a higher level of awareness. Do you think that is what this experience is?"

I lay on my back, staring at the ceiling. The clouds floated by outside, and the sunlight made wavy patterns on the wall. I wasn't going to claim any miraculous consequences of the shark attack—no stigmata, no marks of divine favor. I wasn't feeling it.

"I don't know." I wanted to appear courageous and brave, but I really didn't know.

My thoughts were spinning, the way I used to twirl around and around as a child while staring up into the branches of trees. I couldn't focus. I watched my mind move from image and feeling to image and feeling.

Ron sat quietly next to me, holding my hand as I dozed off.

The nurse came in to check on my meds. I felt the thickness of fresh morphine surrounding me. Ron disappeared. I lay very still and slipped into a half sleep.

There was the smell of meat sizzling somewhere in the building. Beneath it was the pervasive chemical odor of Tilex, Clorox, or 409, but here I felt safe for now thinking about how as a small woman I feared being overpowered by big, aggressive men. I realized I'd learned to use my humor to neutralize my fears.

But in the ocean, it was all different. The ocean didn't care about my gender. In the ocean, there was no power struggle. It was clear who was boss.

That magical world of sea life — it was impersonal. Might makes right was the law of the ocean. And I was missing this day stuck indoors when Maui would heat up to ninety with humidity in the eighties.

I could have been back home in Marin in the midst of winter. The incessant rain. I'd be looking out the living room window. Across the canyon, past the redwood trees, windows lit up through the fog and darkness.

Houses seemed far away, solitary and remote, across the canyon. Everything was sodden as water inked into the earth. Water puddled amoeba shapes on the newly sealed wooden deck. The weatherman predicted more rain and warned to look for fissures in the ground around the foundation of your home. And, "Watch out for trees sliding off of hillsides." I knew our trees were moving. When I looked out our patio door, the redwood and the oak trees were listing to the left. Did they slide when I was not looking?

Neat raindrops pounded the patio and then let up for several minutes, only to resume with full force again. I was immersed in the intense fragrances of the redwood bark, eucalyptus, and bay leaves.

My mind was reflecting on California's extremes — raging fires, mudslides, and earthquakes. The coastline itself hanging like a thin shelf over the Pacific Ocean, ready to break off. After my first earthquake, I had realized how precarious life was there. But I had moved there to escape being subsumed by my mother's judgments, and my father's criticisms of my life. They both were always remarking on where I was falling short.

Other relationships were precarious, too. Specifically, my older brother and me. When he called to say he'd decided to visit with his new wife several weeks before our trip to Maui, he sounded happier than I had ever heard him before. I greeted the news with an old knot of anxiety in my stomach and then felt a surge of excitement about all the things we could do. He had changed since he became a widower and married again.

He had told me that at first, he found it hard to meet a partner because he was in his mid-sixties, retired, and had a lifetime of experiences that left little room for someone else. Yet, out of his loneliness, he was able to make space for a very accommodating woman he met in a widows' club.

In Mill Valley, I wanted to walk with him over the slippery red clay. To have him marvel over the places where nature took over, where we had no control. He did, but it could get tense between us quickly. He made fun of me in front of his new wife. I wondered if she observed how his moods changed rapidly. I never quite knew whom I was speaking to moment by moment. I was still afraid he would shame me, that I would get emotional and start to cry.

When I was in kindergarten, and my brother was in third grade I envied him. He could write cursive and could read. He carried a three-ring binder to school each day. One day I confided. "Kindergarten is so hard. Does it get easier in first grade?" A familiar, closed-lip smile rose above his beefy torso.

"Oh no!" he said. "If you can't do kindergarten, you'll never get to third grade."

As adults, he had ruined a visit to my parents by telling them that I didn't want to come to my dad's seventieth birthday. There were always unsafe places with my brother, and I never knew when one was just a foot or two away—like a fissure in the earth that opened up and I might drop through. Like trees sliding when you turn your back, or an ocean current dragging you out to sea. There were so many events where you could be blindsided.

Lying in the hospital bed, the pain rose, and to take it away I tried to think about something good. I willed my mind not to listen to this persistent pain shooting down my leg and prayed that the drug would kick in soon. I tracked my mind's wandering from image to image, association to association. It landed on a spring day my neighbor died.

As I walked over to his house across the canyon, my mother's Yiddish aphorism for when my life slid off the rails was reverberating off the hillsides: "If you're not worried, something must be wrong." The low whispers of Mom and Dad at the kitchen table after we were in bed, discussing paying the bills, handling a certain run-in with a neighbor, or dealing with the illness of a relative. When all the unforeseen things had been spoken of, they ended the conversation with, "At least we have our health." Hearing their voices downstairs, I felt safe. I didn't know about the impermanence of life then.

Nothing could touch me as a child in their house. The day my neighbor was missing was an initiation. I learned life could take a sudden turn. Something out of the clear blue could touch me. Before cancer, before the shark attack.

After six weeks of relentless rainfall, Hugh Miller went out to check his drains. The hill was chocolate pudding under his feet. It slid right over him while his wife was inside warming up some soup. Did she know where he had gone? Had he told her? Did she think he had clomped downstairs to check the door or to put the car in the garage? Old married couples know each other's habits. If Mr. Miller was out in his garden when I visited, he'd hand me tomatoes. "Take these for your salad. This year they're as sweet as sugar." Mrs. Miller was a small woman in a checkered flannel shirt with a no-agenda face. The day after the slide, when the rain stopped, the sky was a cloudless blue, and by one-thirty the temperature had shot up to seventy-five degrees.

I stood outside my house and took a deep breath of clear air. All the plants, bugs, and weeds had been expecting spring. The no-see-ums swarmed, and there was a sudden riot of wisteria, cherry blossoms, lemon mint, blue bells, and lilies as I walked up the road leading to the hillside overlooking his house. Emergency workers barricaded the street below, digging for him. Some thought he was alive, buried under the mud. Perhaps he was breathing, waiting for the sound of discovery. But it had been fourteen hours since he stepped outside.

Unlike the other side of the canyon, which had few homes and open woods, this side had elegantly refurbished homes with majestic gates. The residents were newcomers. The Millers' side of the canyon was "old Mill Valley," where smaller homes showed signs of weathering and were in need of repair.

I peeled off two layers of wool sweaters. That day, after the storm, the sun was brilliant against a cloudless sky. The only sign of rain was water trickling down the hillside gutters to Blithedale Avenue. As I got closer to the site, I heard the deafening sounds of jackhammers, drills, and backhoes going beep, beep, beep.

There was an urgency to their mission.

A few curiosity seekers stood and looked down past the drop-off where the street cantilevered over the slide. Some of his roof had caved in, revealing a bird's eye view of a dollhouse. Only part of the house was gone. The kitchen had everything in its place: terra cotta covered walls, blue trim, glass cupboards, with plates on shelves, as the restless drone of the shovel crane dug into the mud. searching. His wife had been safely taken to their children's house.

Helicopters from the local television station circled the site with a whirling, deafening noise, dipping and making tighter and lower arcs towards us. I wondered what it was like to be buried by mud. At first, did the old man feel control was only a foothold or an arm's reach away, but when his grasp failed, and with the taste of earth and the ashes in his throat, did he have a moment of recognition? Did he have time to think, "Oh, so this is it?" Like my recognition when the thought flew into my head, "I could die here in the ocean."

The papers said he was a man who knew soil. He was a landscape architect. In the moment that he knew — did he wish he'd had a chance to say goodbye? The sun was baking as I strode past the drop off, hoping to get away from the noise, circle back, and walk down to the front of his house to get a better view. I took my sweater and wrapped it around my waist. Steam from the drying out of the rain mixed with warm sun was rising from the asphalt road. As I walked farther, the emergency work became louder. At the moment I got to the site overlooking the house, the mood had shifted after long hours of digging. The workers kneeling on the roof stood up. A man signaled to the hard hats on the hill who were unfurling the plastic sheeting and securing sandbags with ropes. They stopped their work and gradually, in somber silence, removed their hard hats at the sight below them. The crane ceased pounding, its shovel in midair, with the hoist of mud dribbling but still suspended. At first, the helicopter swooped in closer. Perhaps there was some hope that he might have escaped. Then the helicopter's whirling arc spun in an increasingly larger circle, backing away toward the Golden Gate Bridge, the horizon, and beyond, releasing a wave of relief and horror. The sky was quiet again. It spread out like an expansive soft blue sheet, and we could see past Daly City and down the coast. No-see-ums swarmed at arm's length in mid-air, and the fragrance of wisteria, lemon mint, and lilies filled the canyon. They had found the body below. I wondered how many conversations he'd had with his wife late at night in that kitchen about how they would eventually have to leave each other in death. Life and death seemed so suddenly intertwined with life's impermanence at that moment. It made me wonder if I'd be blindsided someday, too.

12. Wanting My Mother

"YOUR BLOOD PRESSURE IS VERY LOW. I need to change the lines." The nurse leaned over me and fiddled with the plastic tubes going into my arm. Then she worked the digital monitor hanging near my head. Her shadow elongated across the floor in the late afternoon sun. I wanted to reach out and touch her cotton print scrubs with bunnies all over them because I knew they would feel soft. Not like the metal bed, the white wall, the ceiling, and the metal chair that Ron had left beside my bed.

"This will only prick for a moment," she said as she inserted yet another needle into my arm. The blood flowing through the syringe was dark crimson, the color of a silk dress I had long ago. I watched the blood pour into the tube and thought, *people die in hospitals.*

I saw her leave the room, I overheard her call. "I noticed something. You better come as soon as you can."

She came back with a serious look on her face and collected the tape, syringe, and tubing.

Dr. Toma hurried in as the nurse was taking the thermometer out of my ear.

"Her temperature has spiked. She's running a fever," the nurse told him.

"It could be an infection setting in," said Dr. Toma. "We have to get in front of this so we don't have to amputate."

I was taking this very calmly at that moment, because I couldn't absorb it all. Instead, my mind went to observing that the nurse had a strong jaw and strawberry blonde hair, just like my mother, the nurse. I missed her terribly. Not a day went by that I didn't think of her and wanted to talk to her, to ask her advice. "What kinds of things were you dealing with when you were sixty-three?" I was thirty-two when she was sixty-three. There was a thirty-year difference in our ages. I knew her as a mother, but not as a woman. I wish she hadn't suddenly died when I turned fifty. She was proud of being a nurse and having a profession during a time when most women were housewives.

While the doctor and nurse bustled around me, my memory was turning inside out. I was overcome with a sense of destiny. I was letting go of something. A sensation came over me slowly that something important was happening.

There was a new quality to everything around me. Things were floaty, and I was disappearing. I was being carried along.

"Her blood pressure is dropping. Its sixty over forty," I heard the nurse shout.

I felt very relaxed. I didn't have any energy, and I was surrendering to something bigger than myself.

⤺

That night in the hospital, I dreamt about my mother again, but this time I was the age I was in real life and living in Maplewood instead of California. In the dream, I discovered that my mother was still alive, and I was napping in the late afternoon in my upstairs room — the sun slanting low on the horizon, making golden shadows on the wallpaper like it did each autumn on the East Coast. Downstairs in the kitchen, Mom was rooting through the cabinet under the stove, clanging pots and pans while looking for her skillet. Later I heard oil sputtering, and chopped onions sizzling; we were going to have sautéed chicken breasts for dinner with canned marinara sauce. And in the dream, I was my mother's loving, mature, adult daughter, not a rebellious, angry teenage daughter. All the tensions over the years had dissipated.

I was my mother's daughter whenever I visited her in Essex County. It had been the same routine since my dad died. The trip by air was always a long one, starting at six in the morning from San Francisco Airport on a non-stop flight. The Newark skyline in the winter was a chemical silver color in the dusk when I arrived and hailed a cab to rush me the last eighteen miles back home. The driver, usually a Russian immigrant, was often silent during the trip through burnt-out parts of the Newark slums and the brick storefronts on South Orange Avenue. Finally, he pulled up the blacktop driveway, yards away from the front door of the white clapboard house where I had been raised. He would turn to size me up and announce the fare. I always felt gouged. Somehow, I felt this leg of the trip should be free because I knew it like the back of my hand. I would pay him, grab my bag, and climb the front stairs. I knew Mom had heard the taxi. She would have been waiting for hours behind that front door, yet I rang the doorbell formally, as if I were a guest from out of town. (When we were kids, we never used the front door. It was reserved for guests.) The house was cooler when the shades were pulled down because it was an Indian summer this time of year, and the front door was closed. I heard her fumble for the deadbolt, then the chain came out of the latch, and then the door finally unlocked — the symbols of an eighty-year-old woman who lived alone.

She was beaming. I looked into her green eyes. She wore her hairdo like a helmet, carefully coiffed in an unnatural shade of strawberry blonde — a short, sturdy lady from Russian stock who looked younger than she was because of the liveliness in her face.

"Hello, hello. I waited all day for you," she said. A spike of irritation rushed through my body. Love was so complicated.

"I told you I'd be here just after suppertime," I said. Again, my irritation returned and ran through me, followed by anger at myself. Why was I so annoyed at her? There was so much stuff — history, resentments — between us that I wouldn't even know where to begin if I tried to answer that question. It flared up in an instant from some gesture or some familiar sound she made, like licking her lips.

"I warmed dinner up just before I heard you. It's chicken and mashed potatoes, just like you like."

I dropped my bags by the hallway closet, and in a tired drape, I hugged her, pressing against her apron, which hung like a worn sheet from her neck, close to her body. Beneath it, I recognized a muumuu I had bought her on vacation to Maui several years before. She smelled like chicken fat and sweat. I followed her into the brightly lit, tiny kitchen. There, on the table, was my reheated meal. She ran to the refrigerator, grabbed the ketchup, and handed it to me. I always had known that she could read my mind. Suddenly, after all those long-distance conversations financed by phone cards and internet-discounted fees, I was empty of words. I ate in silence. She watched me with an intensity that no one else did in my life. She couldn't take her eyes off of me.

Finally, she asked, "How was the flight?"

"Fine." I kept shoveling the reheated pieces of chicken into my mouth. I had doused them with ketchup because the chicken tasted dry after sitting in the oven, warming, for hours.

I didn't want to look at her. There was so much between us. Things I didn't even know about. We would warm up to one another after a few minutes and then I'd tell her things that I would regret later that night or the next day. But for now, I was home. She wanted to know everything and sat with unflinching attention, listening to the smallest details of my life once I began talking. Words rushed out of my mouth — small talk, important talk, and intimate secrets. I found some perverse joy in describing the dress I saw on sale at Macy's, or the wool Berber carpet I was thinking of buying except that it was too expensive, or the fight I had with Ron before I left the house. She followed my every word, enraptured by my presence. Where else did I have this in my life?

The next day, we went to the Short Hills Mall, part of the weekend-with-Mom routine. Other states had skiing, museums, presidential libraries, or the Liberty Bell—but in New Jersey, shopping was the state sport, and Mom wanted to get an outfit to wear when she visited our distant cousins in Pittsburgh in several months, so we wandered through Saks Fifth Avenue.

"Eleanor said she'd meet us for lunch," Mom said.

When I was thirteen, Eleanor, a friend of my mother's, taught me how to use empty orange juice cans as rollers to straighten my curly hair. When I was sixteen, she coached me on filling out an application for my first job as a receptionist at the Jewish Community Agency because she was a retired social worker.

"Didn't her husband die of a heart attack about five years ago?" I asked. "Wasn't he a criminal lawyer?"

"Yes, he brought some of the Mafia down." Mom laughed. "Just like in *The Sopranos*." We struck a chord between generations.

Suddenly, we saw Eleanor as she lurched across the lobby of Saks, her mules clicking on the faux marble floor. Eleanor liked the dramatic, so in the opposite style from my mom's, Eleanor wore her hair like a Barbie doll, sprayed like she was going to the Academy Awards. Each hair stood in alignment millimeters next to the other in a shocking orange-colored flip. Her scalp was evident as the hairs lined up. Lipstick—I was sure it was Revlon's Red Rose—marked her lips. 1945 was a good year for her lip color. Her look was not exactly an example of keeping up with the times, but I loved the way she bubbled and fawned all over me.

"Honey, you're back. Your mom missed you terribly, and so did I." She pulled me to her and I felt her huge breasts beneath her floral blouse. Many times when I was a kid, I was alternately grateful and ashamed that my mother wasn't as fashion-conscious as Eleanor. "Doesn't she look wonderful!" Eleanor exclaimed, and hugged me again. I was ten pounds overweight—how could I possibly look wonderful? This time I smelled her perfume—strong and expensive. I was fifty years old. I didn't color my hair, much to the disappointment of my mother. "How can I be a strawberry blonde while my daughter has gray hair?" she asked.

I was embraced by this familial situation. We all held hands and walked through the coat department. My mother was on one side, and Eleanor was on the other.

"Remember when you worked here during the Christmas breaks?" Mom asked, reminding me of a memory I'd rather have forgotten.

What I remembered were the cold, dark, long nights when I stood looking at the customers with a smile plastered on my face and counting the minutes before I could go home and take off my shoes. I remembered the relief I felt when I walked out into the thirty-degree cold and saw Eleanor's car, exhaust mingling with the winter night, waiting to pick me up and take me home.

After my mother died and the house was sold, I took what I could fit into my suitcase: three small, handmade needlepoint pillows of wildflowers, a brass candlestick for Hanukkah candles (from before we could afford a real menorah made in Israel), her worn gold wedding band, her favorite challis nightgown, and her address book. These things felt distantly imbued with her vitality. What could I take that would ever bring her back to me whole? I took things that she loved, and these were things that sparked memories of my mother.

There was a time after her death when I needed to talk to her. I kept finding questions that I had failed to ask her when she was alive. I didn't know that I needed them answered until she was suddenly gone. Her address book held the best secrets.

I found it in the top drawer of her nightstand: gold lettering against a red, fake-leather cover. It fit snugly in my hand like a favorite paperback, and, for a moment, I felt like Nancy Drew, discovering a hidden clue about who she really was as a woman, not just my mother. While she was alive, I remember seeing it on the shelf next to the kitchen phone: a rotary dialer with a long beige cord that stretched to the sink, stove, and refrigerator. If she were alive today, I would hear her chirping, "What did we do before cordless phones?" She'd laugh at that, the same way she chirped with her girlfriends—the receiver balanced on her right shoulder while she made supper and waited for Dad to come home from work.

Scrawled in an impatient, cranky script were the names of her friends: nurses that worked in ghetto schools in Newark like she herself did—Miriam, Esther, Sarah, and Rebecca. They had biblical names from another time, not like my friends—Tracy, Ginny, Judy, and Linda. Her friends boasted about their professional daughters and sons, my age, living all over the country—but the lucky ones, unlike my mother, had children and grandchildren who lived close by. At one time, I believed that my mother could see into my mind, and often I felt incontestably crippled by mother-power, which could capture and choke me, so I knew very early on that I had to escape from Maplewood.

When I was in town, her girlfriends included me in their weekly early bird dinners at Edith's Restaurant. Everything on the menu was pureed except for the prime rib. It catered to a geriatric set, and it was the only place in Maplewood where you could gum your food.

"How's your work back in Frisco? Are you writing another book? Where did you buy that lovely dress? When you visit again, we'll throw a party for you. You're just like your mother — she's a very special woman."

I felt embraced and cared for by these women. I imagined that I could come home and be part of their mahjong set, their reading group that discussed Rosamunde Pilcher's latest book, or evening potlucks.

Mom had a fierce energy and exuberance that the others admired. All these women lived alone, where grief was their daily companion. For a while, she was the only one whose husband was still alive, so Dad became the chauffer and restaurant bill checker. The waitress made a big deal of handing him the bill, and he divided it efficiently but understatedly, so as not to offend anyone. The girls — for that's what he called them — often teased him about being the only male at the table: the honorary man. He tucked a pocket calculator into his jacket, and just in case the girls were detained in the ladies' room on the way out, he carried the current Accountants Digest under his arm. After he died, Mom divided up the check.

When Newark was on fire in 1967, and twenty square miles of the city were ablaze, a dozen black parents escorted my mother from her job at Avon Avenue School in the heart of the ghetto safely to the last bus out of the city.

In case of emergency, on the inside page of the front cover of her address book, she listed my cousin Rhoda, my cousin Kenny, my brother, and then she had crossed them all off at various times — the inks were different colors. Maybe she felt angry at them at the time. I could only imagine. And there I still was — not crossed out! I wanted to imagine that I was always the favored one, but I really didn't know.

I turned each page, hoping for something unexpected to pop out: a recognition of something, a clue, an insight, or something I could put together and know finally that all the pieces fit together — that I understood something I had never understood before about her. Emerging from these pages, I wanted some clue to her feelings about her marriage, about her aging, and about her concerns. I couldn't find a hint of anything. She would always be a mystery to me. I flipped page after page, but I didn't recognize some people's names. Maybe this one name was the woman who called me after mom died to tell me that her clothes were ready to be picked up at her alterations shop. I had no energy to pretend by then, so I simply said, "She died." I could hear a silence on the other end of the phone. Then I quietly put the phone back in its cradle. Maybe her name was under "a" for alterations.

So it was with all this in mind—the questions, the longing, and the need for mothering—that I returned months later to close her estate. I planned a tea for the girls, just the way mom would have. I put out her best white linen tablecloth and silverware. The house was up for sale, but we had had no offers yet. Just before the girls got there, I rushed out to the front lawn, dug up the For Sale sign, and dragged it into the garage.

"Your mom always set a beautiful table," Miriam said to me that day.

They arrived in the heat of an August afternoon. We sat in the cool of my mother's living room with the drapes drawn, just the way my mom would have liked it. There were a lot of silences. I saw how each of these women were as broken as I was—needing so much, alone, and frightened. Mom had been without Dad for less than a year, while these women had been living with their aloneness for many years.

Sarah kept referring to her daughter in Florida who won the bread-baking contest, Esther talked about her daughter's cruise to Bermuda with her husband and children, and Miriam said that my dress was very California. The way she said it, I could tell she didn't like the bold blue-and-white print.

That day, they no longer gave focused attention to everything I said. They no longer showed mesmerized interest in me, seemed fascinated by my stories, or adored and idolized me because I looked like my mom, or because I was my mother's daughter. That day, I discovered that the girls were not going to be my new mothers. They didn't say, "If you lived here you could be our fourth in mahjong," and they weren't going to embrace me. I was no longer my mother's daughter. I was a woman who was in my middle years. I was on my own. I was alone. I was an orphan. All bubbling into my longings, memories, and regrets came the question: Would I leave the hospital with one leg?

13. A Visit from a Hawaiian Shaman

I WOKE TO A DAUNTING PAIN shooting up my leg. To my left, a new plastic bag hung above me. To my right sat a stranger with Ron. The stranger was a large man with a barrel chest who didn't look like a tourist. At first I was taken aback, and then I remembered what Ron had said about a man in the lobby of the hospital that wanted to see me. I became curious about his mission.

"Aloha," said the man. "I'm Maxwell. I'm the Hawaiian elder your husband may have mentioned. I came here today to meet you. Your husband ran into me the other day downstairs in the hospital lobby. We talked a little bit, and he said I could visit you. I hope that's okay."

It felt good having a visitor who wasn't a nurse or doctor. It was a distraction from the ache down my leg that would not go away, and all of my meandering thoughts.

"I'm glad to meet you, but why did you come to see me?"

"I read what you said in the paper. Usually when someone gets attacked, they want to go and find the shark and kill it. You averted that by saying what you said."

I was puzzled about his visit, and I felt my typical urge to present myself in the best light. How could I prepare myself, anyway? What would I have prepared any differently than what was here? I ran my fingers through my hair and pulled on the blanket because I knew I didn't look my best. I didn't want him to see my body under the thin green gown. But then my next thought was more reassuring and less self-incriminating—how was I supposed to look? I had been run over by a shark. Still, I thought I had to appear more coherent and more attractive than I felt, but I felt older and more tired from the ordeal. There was a part of me that still relied on my looks and youth beyond makeup and acting cool and relevant, but it crossed my mind—lying in this bed, at this moment with Ron sitting by listening—that I was no longer young, and I was no longer good-looking. I was just an invalid with momentary celebrity.

"Did they find the shark? I mean, my shark?" I asked him, trying to understand why he had wanted to come to visit me; I wasn't operating on all eight cylinders.

"No, but they sent out the usual routine of several helicopters to search for an eighteen-foot shark near the shore. Then they sent the Coast Guard on Ski-Doos, and they've closed the beach down for several days." He paused and looked at my bandaged leg. "They usually don't find the shark, but if they do, they try to scare it farther back out to sea, or kill it.

"My people swim out to meet the Nā 'Amakua when it is time to die." He paused. "I wanted to meet you because of your account in the newspaper. Most people would want to kill the shark. You were respectful of it."

I felt so unequal to the words he had chosen. How could anyone want to kill a shark? Yet, he seemed to have a bigger view than I.

"Eating is part of a shark's job description," I blurted out. Then I felt silly for having said it. I was silently kicking myself because of my quirky sense of humor.

He smiled.

"To those with shark medicine, protection is offered. The medicine and the protection is this: during our lifetimes, we attract events and people we clash with. If there's a situation in your life that you need to resolve, call upon the shark for help. You will be given power and confidence by the shark to fend off negative elements or to get rid of them completely. You know that sharks can never stop swimming, because they have no air bladder. That means that if they stop, they will sink to the bottom of the ocean. "

"That sounds tiring." Another stupid comment, I thought, but I was getting tired of having to be nice to everyone. The comment just slipped out. He didn't seem to mind and went on.

"This is a power animal. They feel the pressure of waves made by a fish in trouble and are also sensitive to electromagnetic waves. They connect us with the creative element of life and water. Throughout Hawaiian lore, water has always been linked with emotional transformation. Sharks reveal to us the strength of the currents of our lives. They see clearly into the murky waters of the future."

"What happens when a shark swims into your life?" Now I wanted to put all the magical stuff aside and get clear as to what this meant to me personally.

Maxwell paused and looked me straight in the eye. He might have looked like any middle-aged man in another situation, but now he looked like a warrior. His sports jacket covered his broad shoulders. Underneath, I saw a standard-issue Hawaiian shirt with broad green leaves and red flowers. He looked nothing like I would have pictured a Hawaiian wise elder, yet he had a gravitas that seemed credible to me.

What if he had come in a headdress and a palm leaf skirt, I asked myself? Would I have some story about that also? I was in a world that I didn't understand.

"The shark gave you a gift. For when a shark swims into your life, this often means that one of the senses is awakened, and visions, prophetic dreams, or clairaudience is possible. This shark will strengthen your emotional muscle."

"My husband said that this was an initiation of sorts. Is he right?" I looked over at Ron, who was listening intently.

I realized that I was feeling uncomfortable in Maxwell's presence. He leaned in and took my hand and smiled warmly at me, as if he knew my anxiety, and I felt myself relax a bit.

"Yes. This is a gift. You've probably had other gifts like this in your life, considering that this happened to you. The shark gave you Shakti Pathi--an energy transmission. You will see, soon enough."

I heard the voice of cynicism in my head. How could losing a leg, getting a life-threatening infection, or leaving Maui with a drop foot be a gift? I wondered anxiously. I was thinking that turning sixty-three and watching some of my friends die or get sick was a loss, not a gift. Discovering the fault lines in my face, the daily aging of my body that was becoming routine, my parents' death, Ron's heart failure — hadn't I had enough loss for the time being? Was this yet another initiation into which my young woman self was becoming the old woman self — a crone?

But there had been a time when I broke through the mirrors of denial and found something transformative about the old woman initiation. In that moment, I left my cynicism behind.

"Maxwell," I said, "I think I've had some initiations before. Do you have to label them initiations? Do you know when they are happening? Or do you learn about them later — maybe upon reflection?"

He smiled. He and I were connecting, and my self-consciousness was disappearing.

"Yes, later in life, you can see that something significant happened, but you may not have known the meaning of it for years and years." He leaned toward me. "Has something like that happened to you?"

"Yes. The year I turned fifty, Ron and I heard of a remote island in the southeast corner of the Dodecanese island chain after we saw the island in a movie called *El Paradiso*. We decided to vacation there," I told Maxwell.

I remember Ron and I flew into Rhodes, and then we left from Mondraki Harbor. In the harbor there were the two bronze stags that guarded the harbor, which drifted out of sight as the boat motored farther out. We looked forward to a week of exploring an ancient island that had a population of two hundred people. It was unlikely we'd run into any American tourists, and we'd have the island all to ourselves.

Within several hours of landing, we ran into a man named Harley and his girlfriend, Lizzie. Harley was a seedy-looking man with a hardscrabble manner, but Ron took to him. Lizzie, his wife, a chain smoker who always had a book in hand, was a wispy Bloomsbury type with an English accent.

The second day, we were sitting at a cafe when Harley said, "A lot of bad shit has happened in these waters." He laughed and snorted. The Aegean Sea spread out before us.

I felt a pang of fear being with this guy. If Ron hadn't taken a liking to him, I didn't think I would be with him alone, but Ron loved to talk to strangers.

Harley told us that during the war, the Italians set fire to the houses to prevent the English from returning and claiming their property.

My instincts told me that he and Lizzie were grifters from the stories Harley had related—living in a Quonset hut in Cyprus, taking ketamine, or going on a bender for several days. Harley was one of the few people who worked on yacht engines of boats that came into the harbor as day boats, so he had access to a lot of boats, and despite his demeanor and being an outsider, he was a valued person on this island because of his skills.

Harley and Lizzie suggested that Ron and I go with them by yacht to a deserted island off the coast of Turkey. Ron jumped at the chance, and I gave a reluctant okay.

As Harley motored the boat out of the semi-circle of the quaint harbor, he told us the history of Kostellorizo. It is in the easternmost part of Greece, and is the most isolated island with only two hundred inhabitants.

"This island belonged to the Greeks, who sided with the Nazis," he told us. "The English bombed the island many times during the war. All the English who lived on this thriving island escaped to Australia."

Lizzie told us that in the last few years, the people who fled returned to reclaim the houses they had abandoned.

I said I hoped we didn't get lost. Harley laughed and showed a row of black teeth.

My stomach was in knots of fear. We were all crowded around the back of the boat, so I couldn't tell Ron what was going on with me without it looking suspicious, but my nausea had turned into seasickness.

"There is land up ahead called the island of Ro. It belongs to Greece, but Turkey tried to invade it during World War II," Lizzie said. "There was an old woman who lived alone on the top of the island. She tended her husband's flocks after he died. She refused to leave during the evacuation and stayed by herself during the war years on the island. Each day, without fail, she put up the Greek flag. We call her the Lady of Ro. The remains of her house are still up there. The Turks tried to get her off the island, but she would outwit them with animal traps—you know, homemade booby traps. They finally let her be and called her crazy, but she was as smart as a fox."

"Whatever happened to her?" I asked.

I remember Harley's smile. "She died only a few years ago. Oh, they just thought she was some brave old woman."

"Is that a good place to go swimming?" Ron asked. The water was deep and clear. As we leaned over the edge of the boat, we could see old, rusted parts of boats, tanks, and jeeps on the bottom. He could tell by the look on my face that I was turning green with seasickness.

"Yes," said Lizzie, "but be careful of the sea anemones. They have fierce spikes, and people can get sepsis if they step on one."

The moment we threw anchor, I jumped off and swam away. I was so glad to get off the boat, thinking that the nausea would stop once I got on land.

The island was uninhabited with low-lying, dead grasses except for a couple of wild goats climbing a well-worn path up the hill.

I scrambled onto the narrow shore and up the hill, following behind the goats and scraping my shins on boulders along the side. Ahead, the two goats didn't look back. I had to see this defiant old woman's house. As my nausea was subsiding, I passed faded scrub, lupine, and followed the animal spore. From above, the ocean was a vast, moving canvas of turquoise and aquamarine. Across the expanse was the coast of Turkey greeting me with cinnamon and warm whites. Behind me, I could see the harbor from where we had motored.

On top of the hill, I reflected that I had just turned fifty and I felt unmoored—as if I'd fallen through a trapdoor in the floor and couldn't find my way anymore. My body was changing with menopause.

As I walked, I found an old stone cistern as warm wind rustled the dried grass. The air was filled with the odor of anise, fennel, and there was a soft buzzing sound in the distance. An old feeling came over me that I'd learned to live with later in life—the sadness of being broken down. By the recent death of both parents and by the aging of my body—a body that had served me so well.

The house Lizzie mentioned was a heap of limestone and slate near a cistern. There was a post from a window on the clay ground, and an old door with a big hole for an old-fashioned metal key. As I looked down into the cistern, I felt the strength of the Greek woman beside me. She was a robust, older woman, and she said, not aloud but in my head, in a voice that didn't sound anything like mine, "Everything is unfolding as it should."

I felt a deep sense of reassurance come over me that I hadn't felt since each of my parents had suddenly died. In that moment, a vista opened up and I could see far into the future with those words.

There was Maxwell still next to my bed. I looked into Maxwell's dark eyes. "I may have to have my leg amputated if I can't get rid of this fever. It's come down a little, though."

Maxwell sat silently. Then he said, "All suffering is bearable if it is seen as part of the story."

I closed my eyes and laid back on the pillow.

I heard him say, "So you see, this is a gift that's been given you."

On the Greek island, I'd closed my eyes, finally knowing momentarily where I was in my inner landscape of life. Vivid before me was the sight of the path narrowing up the hill, with a clump of tree stumps on either side. Now, in the hospital, I felt like I was moving forward on a slow conveyor belt, but encased in memory. The moment seemed still and suspended. After I was gone, there would be no one who knew all of my life. But his new perspective offered me a clarity I hardly had expected.

I was floating and my eyes were closed. How could I be okay living the second half of my life as an amputee?

14. Remembering Botswana

I WOKE IN THE MIDDLE OF THE NIGHT flushed and hot, stuck in panic and dread. I had relived the experience. The shark had ripped my body in two. My head and upper chest were still plotting how to get away, but the lower half—my pelvis, legs, and feet—were drifting over the waves and floating out to sea.

I screamed.

My back ached, and my leg had shooting, red-hot pain.

"Well, dear—it looks like you are having a hard night."

A nurse was standing beside me. There had been so many that I couldn't remember their names. First there was Flora, then Ana, with one N, then Tia, then there was Keshia. After that I stopped trying to remember their names. They were all young, with no hips or breasts: Chinese, Korean, or Hawaiian. Sometimes I couldn't tell because their skin was so smooth and light. Each woman looked thin and fragile.

I felt better knowing that someone was in the room with me, but I felt empty. It was still dark. The drapes were closed. Where was Ron? I was disoriented for a moment. I was lying in a hospital bed and wondering if my leg was going to be amputated. I hadn't slept alone in twenty-five years, and now I was here in a bed situated in the middle of a high-ceilinged, very white room. I had grown sensitive to the different shades of white on the ceiling and could tell the time by how the light slanted in the room.

Back home in Northern California, the wisteria that covered the deck might be showing their little buds. When the flowers bloomed, they looked like white layers of a wedding veil covering the railings that went around the house, softening the brown shingle exterior with two gables and high ceilings. The star jasmine, with its soft fragrance, might have begun winding its vine around the back railing. I thought of how I had found the house while jogging around the block. It was less than an eighth of a mile from our old house, but it reminded me of the dollhouse my grandfather had built for me when I was a child. Now, in the unfamiliar hospital in Maui, I thought—I must remember to ask the doctor when I can go home, spend the night in my own bed, and pet my cat.

"You need some medication to help you sleep," said the nurse. She was prodding my left arm to find a vein in order to put in another supply line.

"I can't find her veins!" I heard her saying frantically to someone else in the room. Her voice was high pitched and wavering. "They've completely retracted. She's dehydrated." I felt the nurses bustling with great purpose. I was aware of every detail.

I felt no emotional attachment to my leg or my body. Every ache and pain was gone. I was floating near the ceiling, watching everything from above.

A medical team arrived and moved with great speed, and there was a sense of urgency in their actions. I couldn't physically feel anything except a release and level of freedom I'd rarely felt.

A rush of air flowed over my chest as a thick curtain was drawn all around my bed. The monitor that sat below my head to the right of the bed silently sent a red line up and down across its screen.

I was in Botswana again in the Peace Corp. It was 1969. A sadness washed over me for a moment. Why had I ever gone to that desolate place? No—it was shame that washed over me.

I felt the shame of lying to my parents about my whereabouts, and leaving them with the task of telling their friends that I was divorced from my first husband after several short years of marriage. No one in my family had ever been divorced before. Later, I learned that they had been so ashamed that they hadn't told relatives for five years. I was ashamed that after studying to be a teacher, I felt like a failure as an elementary school teacher. The shame of disappointing them was almost intolerable. And if that weren't enough, I was living with a man who was neither my husband nor of my religion. What was it about my choices that they couldn't understand?

Dropped into the dry, hot, and dusty village of Molepolole with Doug, my boyfriend, our life together changed drastically from the noise, excitement, and the activism of Berkeley. Every day back home, something was happening on Telegraph Avenue: conga drumming, sit-ins, or street venders selling their homemade jewelry. In Botswana, there were no other people around to lessen our loneliness, and we found ourselves inextricably together day and night. This wasn't exactly the career changer I'd hoped for, but I'd had to find a way to leave teaching and find work that I actually enjoyed. It was 1968, and the Peace Corp promised a career in community development—whatever that was. It sounded interesting, and what the Peace Corps offered was the first opportunity that emerged. At first, the country we chose seemed like a sudden shock, and then a self-imposed exile.

"The English doctor thinks I'm pregnant because I haven't gotten my period for three months," I told Doug one day.

Doug sat in the only chair in the hut, sucking hard peppermint candies and reading science fiction paperbacks day after day. After a long silence, he said, "Let's go see the Peace Corps doctor when he comes out here."

I felt relieved that he had a plan for us because at that moment I was too upset to think of what to do besides sit down and cry my eyes out.

Outside, the sun scorched the desert to 110 degrees during the day—hot, harsh, and unyielding. At night, we lay under three blankets and mosquito netting as the temperature dropped to thirty-two degrees.

Each day was like the last. It began at 6 a.m., unlike the late mornings after we'd stayed up late in Berkeley smoking dope and listening to music. In Botswana, I made food in a three-legged iron pot over an open fire. This pot, a wooden ladle, and a spatula were our only cooking utensils. For the Motswana, this was a way of life. Each morning, they pounded the millet grain or sorghum with a large mortar and pestle, then cooked their daily meal.

During the first few months, several Motswana showed up wanting to work for us. "All Americans are rich," I frequently heard. A British volunteer named Bruce explained that hiring them was the only civil thing to do in a country where no one could get any work. We employed Mohohaballi, Sheito, and other villagers to fetch water by digging in the riverbeds that had been dry for a decade and to carry the water on their heads several miles to our hut, or to sweep the dirt floor and wash our dishes.

Every day, Motswana flocked to our hut, which served as a newly-formed handicraft center. A local teacher turned the hut into a buzzing hive of activity of sewing, making pottery from local clay pits, and crocheting.

I had made the director of the program for the country promise that I wouldn't have to teach school, so I became a community developer. However, no one knew what my job was. I didn't know what I was supposed to do, because I didn't understand the culture, the heat slowed me down, and I couldn't learn the language fast enough.

I had brought a toolbox filled with leather tanning tools that weighed over twenty pounds. I was to start my new career tanning leather from goats and cattle. Someone would teach me. The box sat on the shelf unopened. The Kalahari bush men cured their leather using urine. When I took out my toolbox and opened it, they went slack-jawed for lack of understanding of how to use these tools. When they tried, a few hours later I found them returning to their own wooden spatulas and urine.

Time slowed down in this part of the world that was seventeen hours away from California by plane. We were young and looking for adventure. It wasn't about JFK and patriotism — we were too self-centered for that in our twenties. Doug, too, was having difficulty finding satisfying work in the states. The sky remained a flat blue day after day. No rain was in sight. I was a city girl — put me in the desert and spiders, iguanas, and bobcats become the enemy.

"The doctor gave me a blood test, but the vials broke in the lorry to the capital city," I reported back to Doug after a week of waiting silently and worrying. It had been too long, and I'd heard nothing.

I dragged myself over to the compound in a low-lying building beside a makeshift hospital. I was the only white woman sitting in the rickety chairs outside on the porch waiting to see the doctor, and once again I took a blood test.

Although it seemed like everyone liked Americans in 1968, the U.S. government had poor relations with South Africa. I could feel that the doctor, an older South African man, had no good feelings for me, because of my lifestyle — living in sin with a man. Nor did the nurse who administered the blood test yet again.

"You should be ashamed for getting yourself into this," she said as she poked me hard with the needle.

I knew if I mouthed off, I wouldn't get my blood test, so I sat quietly and took it in.

Meanwhile, I was feeling sicker and sicker. I climbed the ladder to our loft bed with a chamber pot beside it and stayed there under the mosquito net.

One day, a hissing noise began very slowly. At first, I thought it was the sound of a youngster singing on the floor below the loft where I slept. Then I heard the women's voices in a hushed panic. Soon they were taking in all the pads and blankets and pots and food that were lying outside. The sound got louder and louder. From the window, I could see the horizon turning a dark brown. At first, I thought there was a storm coming our way. Then the sound became deafening, and with it came huge, brown, winged bugs — thousands of them now filled the sky. Suddenly, there was no more sky. I understood what the brown was: it was a locust invasion. We were in the path of a locust plague. I dove under the mosquito netting and hid under the covers. The locusts were coming in through the thatch and filling the house. They lay scattered on the dirt floor, covering the mosquito netting, sitting on the chair, the tables, and hanging on the walls. And just as quickly as they appeared, the locusts disappeared. The dead ones covered everything in sight, both indoors and out.

The women came out from their hiding places with great commotion and joy. Before my eyes, they scurried around, building a great bonfire in the middle of the desert. Then they collected mounds of locusts, grilled them, and ate them gleefully.

Finally, I came down from the loft. My stomach clenched as I was offered and ate a handful of locusts. They tasted like some soft flesh with a crispy skin. I forced them to go down my throat, while I nearly choked, leaving my throat scratchy and raw. I was left with an aftertaste that wouldn't go away for hours. But to the community, eating a grilled locust was like an ice cream treat—a treat for them after the wearisome millet twice a day.

People could see that I was growing weaker and yellowish. As I lay in bed, I reviewed the brief twenty-seven years I'd been on earth. I simply could not take in the sights, sounds, smells, and life-surviving behaviors that surrounded me. I needed a time out. I got very sick.

A week later, Doug came into our hut and told me that he ran into the doctor from the hospital, who told him that my tests came back negative. I was relieved to know that I wasn't pregnant, but I continued to feel sick.

One morning in July, we saw in a news magazine that men had landed on the moon. Doug showed all the workers at the handicraft center the article in a month-old Time magazine. They were incredulous.

"But the moon is up in the sky," one said. "This cannot be true." It was as incomprehensible to them as it was to me to wash my hair in a bucket of cold water, cook over an open fire, or live in a hut with no electricity—or why I had ever come to Botswana. Or how come I was so thin. In Botswana, if you were rich—as all Americans were—you were supposed to be corpulent. One Motswana asked me if I was a convict who had to flee from America. It made no sense to them why anyone would come and live in their village. Why was I so thin? Had I been a fugitive?

They also questioned a photo on a page of the magazine of black children in fake fur coats drinking subsidized milk in a Bronx school program.

"Look at those fur coats. Children wear fur coats in America. They must be very rich."

I explained to them that the coats were fake fur, but I couldn't get the concept across to them. It was like when I asked them why an old Motswana lady was going around screaming.

They said, "Because she is old."

"Does she have something wrong with her body or brain? Is she sick?

"No, she is old."

In Setswana there were no words for psychological conditions. No concept of people being on the moon or children wearing fake fur.

What I missed the most — that I'd always taken for granted — was the ocean. Out the door of our hut, all you could see for miles was sand and the blurry lines of heat rising from the desert. I would stand there for hours and try to imagine that at the end of the horizon was the ocean, if I could just walk that far.

And why was I now going back in time to relive this earlier experience? My mind was like a digital reference librarian whom I only had to call up to ask, "And what other experiences do you remember like the one you are having now?" and boom — they appeared across the movie screen of my mind.

In Maui Memorial, the doctor poked his head in the door. I didn't know whether it was day or night. The doctor had sat down with me briefly to explain the leg amputation procedure — "If it comes to that," he had said. And he didn't volunteer his little medical school lecture about amputation on his own — I had to reassure myself that I had pulled it out of him.

Again, here in Maui, I was in a situation that I didn't want to be in, with people who were not my tribe, and with an outcome — like pregnancy — that I didn't want to have, because of something I did without realizing the consequences: leg amputation.

In the Peace Corps, I slowly began to see that this wasn't my tribe. I wasn't as resilient as I thought: to be dropped off anywhere — I could survive perhaps, but flourish, no. The pregnancy test had come back negative, and I was relieved, but when I got back to California, I was diagnosed with hepatitis. I had survived, but I needed both a plan and confidence to move forward in my life. Childhood was over, and I couldn't delay maturity any longer. And when I returned to California, I had a plan for myself. I was going to become an adult.

15. Another Encounter – Breast Cancer

LYING IN MY HOSPITAL BED, I had a lot of time to look back at sixty-three years. I was amazed at all the time I'd lost trying to find my way. Over the years, I was able to show myself some compassion: little things like forgiving myself for not having the inner resources when I was seven or twenty or thirty to make good decisions, and taking what I learned from my fears of my brother, the shame my mother and father must have felt at my choices, and the fear of not fitting into a conventional life. But how the hell could this shark attack have happened to me? It seemed so random, in its way.

One morning I caught a glimpse of myself in the mirror. There I was—a gray-haired, petite woman whose face was lined with wrinkles. Why hadn't I ever seen her before? Ron called my wrinkles a map of the joys in my life. I called them wrinkles. Some of my girlfriends looked so much younger than I did, with their faces pulled back into their hairlines, looking tortured: dyed hair, pancake makeup, and a ponytail face lift. Johnny Carson once said at the *Academy Awards*, "It's so good to see so many new faces on the old faces."

Each of us had things we were deeply embarrassed by, and liked to think we'd cunningly them concealed from the world—but which were, in fact, pitifully obvious. Most of the time other people didn't understand why our embarrassment was such a big deal and could cause us so much shame, but it was a big deal to us. I could tell by our inept and transparent efforts to cover up the embarrassment. How did one cover up wrinkles? I for one was oblivious to them until my sister-in-law reported to a friend, "She looks very well dressed, except for those wrinkles on her face." I pretended not to hear, but from that moment on; I felt shame when walking into a room filled with strangers.

Meanwhile, no news was forthcoming from Doogie Howser, but a nurse had alluded to the fact that between shifts, some nursing staff had dropped the ball and let me get dehydrated, because the previous shift had forgotten to change the empty saline bag. That triggered low blood pressure. Luckily, another nurse discovered me languishing. My fever finally abated with a new course of full spectrum antibiotics.

Here I was, unexpectedly in a bed in a hospital and my story daily covered in the print, social media, and television in the local, state, and national news. What must people have thought of me when they saw me on the news? I had written four books, worked hard to get a doctorate degree, and built a business as an entrepreneur for twenty years. Now I was the potential poster icon for *Shark Gal of the Year* by doing nothing but being in the wrong place at the wrong time. All my other hard-earned accomplishments didn't even seem to merit notice.

Then there was Maxwell's visit. It got me thinking. His name didn't fit his role as a kahuna. Instead it made me think of a Beatles' song. Surely Maxwell wasn't a Hawaiian name. If he were really a kahuna, wouldn't he have some long, complicated Hawaiian name? When Ron told our friend Jake about Maxwell's visit, Jake said, "He is the real deal." That made me feel a little better.

Gina dropped in to visit with a pint of ice cream and one snorkeling fin. "Hi. I don't mean to pop in unexpectedly, but I found this one fin on the beach and thought the shark—your shark—had spit it out."

She threw back her blonde hair, with her blues eyes sparkling as she laughed at her own joke.

"Ron already tried this prank. Let's put it on the bookcase. We can use it for the Shark Altar," I said.

She took the beach-worn fin and placed it right smack in the middle of the bookcase. I wondered how many other fins I'd get before this was over.

"Well, you are quite a celebrity I hear. Every time I turn on the news, there you are giving another interview."

"Actually, a nurse had told me that several radio talk show hosts have called the hospital to talk to the 'lady that was attacked by the shark.'"

But I was not in a state to talk to anyone at that moment except Gina.

Gina and I had been friends for decades, but I was noticing how a strange thing had happened as we both moved into our sixties. We were becoming increasingly aware of the finite nature of time, the choices we had made, and the narrowing of options remaining to us. I sold my bicycle after I fell off it and tore my rotator cuff. After I was diagnosed with osteopenia and arthritis, I gradually gave away my favorite pairs of high heels. In retrospect, I wondered how I could have walked all day in those shoes for years at my job in San Francisco.

But today I saw myself doing something else: I was judging my peers and the choices they had made in their lives. My reactions ranged from envy to resentment. I found myself anxiously sizing up how everyone else's decisions had worked out in order to reassure myself that my own choices were vindicated. That I, in some sense, had won. But this setback made me feel anxious and ashamed at not getting out of the shark's way.

And so it was with Gina. When we first met in our thirties, we were like identical seeds — we were both into clothes and men. Now we looked at each other with ironic incomprehension. She had moved to Maui, married a wealthy real estate developer, and lived a vacation lifestyle like most of her girlfriends. They dressed in flowing thin muumuus and called themselves goddesses or mermaids. Their husbands supported them. I, on the other hand, had worked as a college professor and owned my own consulting business. I had learned in the previous decades that no one was going to rescue me. Even husbands are not in the rescue business. Unlike Gina, I had to rescue myself — and then I learned to like doing it. And just as I'd done during the shark attack, I'd done a damn good job of it.

"I heard you on the television news last night. You sure haven't lost your sense of humor even in the face of disaster," she said as she moved the chair closer. Two spoons appeared and the lid came off the ice cream as we each took turns passing the carton and taking mouthfuls of Jamoca Almond Fudge.

"The more anxious I am, the funnier I seem to find myself," I admitted to her. Inside, I was thinking about how this forced inertia was one of those occasions when you have to forget the upcoming month you had planned to spend out in the world, and accept that what you're going to be doing is nothing. You'll see a doctor who shows up for four minutes a day, calls that medical care, and then runs off unceremoniously.

Gina, Fuzzy, Wes, Natalie, Della, and Marvin had become the kind of family I always wanted, and over the years Ron and I had deepened our relationships with each of them, both as couples and as individuals.

Gina was a reassuring presence, so much so that I simply closed my eyes and — with the help of all that sugar from the ice cream — drifted off.

When I awoke later, Ron was sitting there. A diagonal beam of sunshine crossed his cheek and torso. He leaned toward me and kissed me on my forehead like I was a little girl.

"Good morning, Sleepyhead. How do you feel?"

I looked. Both legs were still there. Ron looked at the same time, and we both laughed.

Hospital stays were one of the few times in adulthood when we had an excuse to drop all busywork that normally preoccupied us and go be with the people we loved, or just surrender if you were a victim, like myself. You simply spent time with loved ones, no special occasion required — such as a wedding or anniversary, dinner or theater. You just sat there in the same room, making small talk or reading, offering the dumb comfort of your presence. You were literally There For Them.

Ron had been there for me before, during a crisis early in our marriage. It was 1990. I had stopped into my gynecologist's office for an annual appointment, but I was going now. I was very caviler about this visit — things were going well in my life. All feelings of well-being came to a grinding halt when Dr. Beso, during a manual breast exam, found a lump in my right breast the size of a pea. I had hit my first big speed bump at age forty-eight.

Back then, there was little information available about the breast cancer epidemic. I was diagnosed the month that George Bush, Sr. and Mikhail Gorbachev were declaring that the cold war was over — but my personal cold war was just beginning.

All of a sudden, Ron and I thrust ourselves into the medical-industrial complex: the world of mammograms, biopsies, ultrasounds, and fine needle aspirations. Each surgeon had a different suggestion about recovery, but they all voiced the same opinion: I needed a double mastectomy. My husband asked one female doctor, "If these were your breasts, what would you do?" She replied, "Oh, I'm past my childbearing years — I don't need these jugs anymore. I'd cut them off." At that time, we were met with a callousness from doctors who were formerly general physicians, who hadn't understood that these body parts were not just something out of an anatomy class, like a pig to dissect in biology class. At that time, the doctors were mostly old white men used to performing general surgery to remove livers, colons, or stomachs. I had fallen into feeling like a victim of the medical labyrinth after several months of anticipating the surgery. We did find one male doctor who was willing to give me a right breast lumpectomy. We chose him.

My parents were adamant about coming out from New Jersey and helping me through the surgery and recovery. "You know, some children don't have parents who are our age, who are well enough to fly out and help you," my mother told me.

I wanted them to be with me, but knowing my mother, I wondered if I wouldn't be taking care of them instead. She confirmed this by asking, "Do you have a toaster? I noticed you didn't have a toaster the last time we visited. Dad likes his bread toasted in the morning."

Ron and I had only been married for five years, and we hadn't completely bonded yet.

I knew it wouldn't be unlike my parents to hop on a plane and surprise us, so I didn't tell my mom when the surgery was scheduled. At the same time, they wanted us to come back for my Dad's eightieth birthday a week after my surgery.

"I feel so guilty, but I don't want them here," I told Ron.

One evening a week prior to the scheduled surgery, I flew up to Portland to meet my husband after he did some consulting work at Intel Corporation. I normally didn't do this because I was working, but the impending surgery was approaching, and we both felt a sense of urgency to spend more time together. We had gone out to eat at a little Indian restaurant, and as we were walking back to the bed and breakfast where we were staying, he said, "I will miss you if you die. I love you so much — I can't imagine my life without you."

It was dusk, and the sky had turned a shade of lavender. It was the time of year when cherry blossoms scattered the sidewalk. I looked down at our feet shuffling through the blossoms and felt a sudden surge of renewed energy — angry energy.

"I'll be damned. I'm not going to die! I'm not going to let another woman drive my convertible, use my computer, or sleep in our bed with you."

"In that order?" he asked. We both laughed.

In that moment, I had regained my power.

"I'm not going to be bullied by cancer."

The day of the surgery, we were ushered into an elevator with fifty other people in patient gowns who were accompanied by their families and taken to separate, curtained cubicles. I burst into tears as I took off my clothes, put them into a plastic garment bag, and for the last time said goodbye to part of my right breast as I knew it. The surgeon's words during the preparation that morning were, "We never really know what we've got until we get right down into it." Ron pulled me toward him and held me.

"Remember — you are not going to be bullied by cancer."

I lay on the gurney in the cold room. The anesthesiologist opened the curtain and tried patiently to find my vein to put in a port. Only curtains separated patients from one another. Next to me, not a foot away, was an elderly man talking to his son about his heart operation. On the other side of the opposite curtain was a man being comforted by his son and daughter in Chinese. We were all lying on our gurneys, awaiting the surgeries that could change our lives.

A nurse came in.

"We are almost ready," she told me. Then she addressed Ron. "You can walk to the end of the hall with the team of doctors who will perform the surgery. Then you must turn left and go into the waiting area, and we will turn right."

She pushed the curtain open, and three doctors appeared. As the attendants wheeled me down the hall, Ron put a surgical blue paper cap on my head and gently tucked my hair under it. "Now you are a part of the team."

Time disappeared. Waking up after surgery I felt cold and nauseated. Nurses were scurrying around to help. Ron was always in sight.

That night, I dreamt that Ron's mother, who had died several months earlier, was helping me carry a garment bag full of my possessions somewhere to be safe. These were clothes made of silk, leather, and furs. Joanne was a good helpmate and friend. We were putting them in a car, and the clothes were heavy. She suggested that I might no longer need these because I was struggling with them, but I persisted. There was a sense of striving in the dream. I was traveling up a long winding road and it was dark, like in the dead of night. I sensed many people along the way, encouraging me and helping me. I sensed my mother and father looking on, evaluating the situation, and feeling satisfied with what they saw; but they were hurt that they couldn't pitch in and be a part of it.

Ron slept on a cot in the room that night.

The doctor reported that the surgery was unremarkable. It was the first time in my life that "unremarkable "was remarkable to me.

Since that time I was vigilant, that every May I marched myself into the gynecologist's office and made an appointment for my yearly mammogram. And every year, a week later, I'd get a letter in the mail telling me that my mammogram had been normal. My old doctor had since retired, and a lovely Latina doctor had taken over his practice. I missed how my old doctor and I would joke around together while he was examining me under the white sheet and my feet were in stirrups. He had found the lump after having stayed up for twenty-four hours delivering a baby at a hospital nearby.

"Why do nurses give old men in hospitals Viagra at bedtime?" I once asked him.

He looked up from under the sheet. "Why?"

"So they don't roll out of bed at night."

I'd gotten mammograms, allowing generously endowed women to make tacos out of my little breasts as they squashed them into the metal machine.

In 2017, I didn't get my annual follow-up letter. I got a phone call when I was just about to buy some pricey sandals at Nordstrom.

"We've detected some abnormal cells," said the nurse on the other end of the line. "Your mammogram doesn't look normal. We'd like you to come in for another mammogram."

I abandoned the purchase and ran outside the store. The dry, warm air of the summer day hit me like a brick. I looked up at the flat, blue California sky. My phone beeped. A friend had tweeted another tweet. Nothing had changed, but my life had taken an unexpected turn.

Now there was a new checklist to complete: make an appointment for another mammogram to be sure the first one wasn't a false positive, schedule an ultrasound, a biopsy, and then an MRI. The tests all confirmed what the doctors and I instinctively knew: it was DCIS—ductal carcinoma in situ.

Twenty-seven years before, when I had had a lumpectomy, all the surgeons were old white men with fingers like the sides of beef. They were used to hoisting kidneys and colons out of other old white men. They would say things like, "How do you think you did this to yourself?" I felt humiliated.

Now I was an identified patient on the biopsy, ultrasound, and MRI conveyor belt. It became very evident that I needed a mastectomy with or without reconstruction, or a lumpectomy with radiation.

Sitting in the examining room with the first breast surgeon, I asked, "Don't I get extra credit for all my years of normal mammograms?"

The surgeon smiled briefly and discussed my options. A lumpectomy would be challenging because the ductal carcinoma in situ was meandering in a seven-centimeter area. With a lumpectomy, radiation was required every day except Sundays for six weeks.

It was the radiation that frightened me. With a mastectomy, there would be no radiation, chemotherapy, or tamoxifen.

"What happens if three months from now I hate the way I look without a breast?" I asked the doctor.

"With a mastectomy and no reconstruction, there is no going back to get reconstruction later. We've already rid you of the nipple and the surrounding skin," he replied. In my mind, I pictured him taking my nipple and skin and making a hoop shot into the trash can. "But with a mastectomy and immediate reconstruction, you can change your mind later."

There were no good choices. It felt like I was losing a limb. The surgery was scheduled six weeks out.

That was in the past. Now, looking at my bandaged leg, I wondered—would I once again lose another limb?

16. Breast Cancer – Redux

I TOLD ONLY MY CLOSEST FRIENDS about the breast surgery. I started looking at women's breasts — in the locker room, in the pool, and in yoga class, appreciating mine for the first time in my life. I was breast shopping. Why do some look good on some women and not on others? "It's symmetry and volume," one surgeon told me.

"They have served you well and taken you a long way," another breast surgeon said.

I had always been flat chested, so I decided long ago to ignore my breasts. When I began to swim, my upper body became more defined and stronger. I filled out. In the sixties, the fashion was mini-skirts, not plunging necklines, and I focused on my brain. Although I may have ignored my breasts much of my life, that didn't mean that I wanted to sacrifice one.

For six weeks, I alternated between abject terror and at least once a day putting my head down on a table and sobbing into my hands so hard that my body shook. I hadn't cried in that kind of soul-shattering way since I was a kid. I used to frighten myself just by sobbing alone, but as I got older, it felt good to let myself go.

Friends tried to comfort me by saying, "You'll get through this. You've gotten through worse." But that didn't help. I couldn't imagine life after the surgery date.

One friend reminded me, "Woody Allen said, 'I don't mind death, I just don't want to be there when it happens.'"

And that's just the way I felt: jokingly, but also terrified.

When my mother was alive, I always admired her practical side. When bad things happened to me, like getting sick and being confined to bed, instead of comforting me with words of kindness, she'd say things like, "Well, it's better than being stuck in the eye with a sharp stick." Or, "Would you rather be in solitary confinement for forty years?"

The strange way I comforted myself was to follow her legacy and reassure myself — perversely so — by thinking about the immigrants that have had to swim the Rio Grande to get to the United States, or the soldiers fighting in

Iraq, or the starving babies and the helpless look in the eyes of the Ethiopian mothers. Yup, I'll take a mastectomy with reconstruction. It would be a two-for-one deal. If I didn't like myself with the mastectomy after three months, I couldn't go back because the skin and nipple would have been thrown into some hospital dumpster. But, if I took the mastectomy and immediate reconstruction and I didn't like how my breast looked, I could come back and they could take the silicone donut out of my right breast. After all my self-loathing, there was still self-loathing, no matter how you looked at it.

My niece came up with an invaluable solution. "Why don't you give your breasts a name and personality—then you could have a conversation with them to help them through this awful waiting time?" Her drama therapy training was proving its value.

Brilliant. The names came to me while watching the latest chaos in the White House on CNN. The left healthy breast was named *Melania,* and the right breast where the surgery would occur was dubbed *Ivanka.* They both were lovely women, to be sure. Melania was self-contained and savvy about staying alive (and being taken care of financially). She knew her place in the scheme of things. Ivanka, a bit clueless on the other hand, had to accept her fate.

So with this new awareness, I was able to struggle through the surgery and the endless recovery. I was grateful that this had happened when I was past the dating game, that Ron reassured me by reminding me that he loved me for who I was, and not what I looked like, and that my friends were kind and willing to help out. Carol brought her favorite veggies, Claire snuck over a sheet cake just like the one Tina Fey made famous, and Jeri filled my inbox with cute cat videos she knew I would love.

By the time I'd reached this age, I had become used to appearing invisible to men. That was what happened at this stage of life. Old men looked at young girls. Being invisible had some advantages. Mainly, I stopped caring what others thought, and I was grateful that my time was my own after all those years of working to make a living and trying to be liked. But the main thing I was learning was that I wasn't my body. And that was a hard one. I'd taken my body for granted for so many years. That was a lot of wine, potato chips, and ice cream that I had consumed over the years—fatty foods that led to cancer. Even with reconstruction, I knew I wasn't going to look like Pamela Anderson from Baywatch. I was accepting of my fate.

One night, I ran across a quote from Joseph Campbell: "Opportunities to find deeper powers within ourselves come when life seems most challenging."

That sounds great when you are at the top of your game, but what happens when you are at the bottom?

When friends learned the news, some began behaving strangely. One took me aside to tell me that she had always admired my grit and creativity. She loved how I was such a straight shooter, and that I was just what I appeared, with no games. Another hugged me, trying to avoid hurting my Ivanka, who was healing from two needle biopsies, an MRI, and lots of prodding and pulling from the tacos-under-the-mammogram-machine. Another artist friend, known for her reserved nature, told me that she had always admired my paintings, and wished she could paint like me.

At one point, I blurted out, "I'm not going to die. I will probably wake up from the surgery, so save this for my eulogy at my memorial service." What was this memorializing really about? Why did some people withhold the good thoughts, secret envies, and admirations until they thought it was going to be their last shot with you?

There was a new generation of women surgeons. Having a female surgeon was mainstream now. Times had changed, and attitudes had changed since the lumpectomy in 1990. There was now a whole building devoted to breast cancer recovery at The Cancer Institute in Kentfield, California. It felt like going into a spa. The hallways were light and airy.

There was a new role called patient navigator that had not existed back when I had my first surgery. I had my own personal patient navigator! She led patients through the maze of forms, insurance, and scheduling. (I imagined she was going to row me down the River Styx like a gondolier, helping me find my way through the rough waters of the hospital bureaucracy and onto the operating table. I use this metaphor because I was certain I would not wake up. I'd read about Joan Rivers' death in the hospital.)

Volunteers were falling all over themselves with their specialties to help me. Two sweet, older women made heart-shaped pillows by hand to give to breast surgery candidates. Some held free tai chi classes, chi gong, guided imagery, and massage therapy. You could practically matriculate at the Marin Cancer Institute and get a degree in mastecology. I left the center with a tote bag filled with essential oil body lotion, two plush, heart-shaped pillows, several bottles of scar-eliminating lotion, hand sanitizer, and two camisoles made expressly for fake boobies. I felt like I'd won the lottery.

⌐⌐

A month before the surgery, I was not in my right mind. I was talking to myself all the time. I'd signed up for a right breast mastectomy with a female surgeon, with immediate reconstruction by a male reconstructive surgeon. Several times a day, I'd have a sudden shocking thought, "Guess what? I have breast cancer. I'm going to have surgery." Then I talked myself down by a reassuring thought: "Just think, it will be followed by immediate reconstruction. I get to go home with a new right breast, and I couldn't have found a better time to have stage 1 cancer." That was irony. That was my personal cynical humor. I was in the slow lane as a retired person, and it was the dog days of summer, when things were held in suspended animation.

I spent the time before my surgery organizing my clothes closets, rearranging my computer devices and cables, and going through my files. I had done this numerous times before, and I couldn't believe that I'd found yet an even better way to organize my already-organized stuff. I almost began alphabetizing the soup cans on the shelves in the pantry. Time had slowed down when I wanted to speed it up and get this over with.

Among my precious things were twenty pairs of clunky earrings designed by Tabra circa 1988, ten beaded necklaces that I'd recently seen at a flea market, and my two old computers.

I looked around the house. There was nothing to steal in our house. Everything was old and worn out, including the occupants.

Why was I organizing worthless stuff? It seemed to quiet the chaos going on in my head. What if I didn't wake up after surgery? What if there were an unanticipated surprise? Had I done enough research and asked all the right questions?

As the days wore on in a fog, I wrote a brief note to Ron and stuck it in my desk drawer in the hopes that he'd find it there in the event I died on the operating table. They were instructions for my memorial service. "Please play Aretha's 'Pink Cadillac,' The Rolling Stones' 'Brown Sugar,' and don't forget Barry White's 'I Can't Get Enough of Your Love Baby.'"

The night before surgery, I wasn't sure I'd wake up on time in the morning, so I set my iPhone for 7:00, 7:30, and 8:00 a.m. I woke up before any alarms went off. The streets were empty as Ron drove me to Marin General. We didn't have to face the Monday morning garbage trucks as we wound our way around and down the mountain. The streets seemed strangely empty for this time of day. We were both silent.

⏛

I woke after the surgery in a double room. My bed was near the door. Across from me sat my husband and his best friend. In the fog of after-surgery, they seemed very entertaining until they left at four o'clock that afternoon.

By then, the drugs had started to wear off, and the woman in the bed separated from mine by a curtain introduced herself and her visiting son and daughter to me. I made the mistake of asking her what she was in there for, and she began unraveling her medical history as if I were a doctor taking notes. I dozed off. Luckily, she couldn't see me from the other side of the curtain.

After I woke later, I began to feel very nauseous. The nurse gave me a small, kidney-shaped plastic bowl to use, but I missed the perimeters by a mile. Meanwhile, the woman in the bed behind the curtain had gotten up to nineteen-ninety in her medical history.

A short time later, the nurse came running in because she heard my cries for help, and she shoved a plastic pan under my nose the size of a baseball field. Meanwhile, the neighbor's family silently slipped out one by one, as if finally realizing that something untoward was happening in the next bed that could reach critical proportions.

When I was a child, my parents used to take long Sunday drives from New Jersey to upstate New York to "see the trees and flowers," my mother would say. I guess it was comparable to a "staycation" of nowadays because we didn't have a television back then.

I was known in my family as "the hurler." My dad would patiently stop the car. My mom would get out of the back seat with me, and I'd retch and retch. She'd smile and say, "You're like Johnny Appleseed. You're fertilizing the wild daisies."

I had felt so much shame around vomiting that as an adult in the hospital, when I had this crisis of monumental proportions, even with anti-nausea medication, I tried to do it elegantly, but I couldn't, so I just let it rip. More family exited from my neighbor's side of the room.

Within twenty-four hours, I was at home resting with two drains tucked into a camisole with a kangaroo pocket that had been given to me by the volunteers. Every twelve hours, I had to pour each drain into a small bottle with marks on the side to measure the output. I had to keep a diary of the time and date and amount. At first I was resistant to do this because of the "ick" factor, but Ron stepped up and showed me how to do it. After that, I really got into it and made an extra column on the paper for the color. The doctor told me that liquid would start out red and go to yellow, and then the drains could come out. In response to that, I thoughtfully gave each measurement a color name. The first day, the liquid was pinot noir. Slowly it became rosé, and a week later it turned to chardonnay. That day, the doctor took the drains out, and he couldn't resist showing his nurses my creative endeavor.

When I explained my extra column on the paper for the color, Ron laughed and said, "I love how you make everything into an art project."

After surgery, I spent two weeks lolling around. No lifting, pulling, driving, exercising, or errands—just lying in bed with my cat. I began making lists, as if the lists themselves had arms and legs and could reach out and complete the tasks that I'd assigned myself. I relaxed into recovery. I had learned how to heal. I learned that after the boredom runs its course, creativity begins to grow in the unexplored soil. I was painting pictures in my head, and mind-mapping stories of episodes I remembered from my past. I was required to do nothing but heal day after day, and my life as I knew it returned with new vigor.

I couldn't swim for six weeks, and swimming helped me from having mini mental meltdowns. Without swimming or other exercising, I had a lot of time on my hands. Between driving to Harbor Point, swimming for an hour, showering, and returning home, it took up a better part of the day. I was getting used to being in the slow lane—although it felt more like a ditch. I returned my pre-surgery books to the library and resumed reading more balanced literature as well as writing in my journal.

My energy flagged in the afternoon—as the surgeon had said it would do.

"Give yourself six weeks with no lifting, walking, or exercise," she had said.

However, every morning after the drains were out I sprinted from the bed to the shower, filled with energy. I had survived the surgery, been given a new Pamela Anderson from Baywatch breast (well, not as big), and my very own nipple had been preserved. My new breast matched the other one perfectly. Life was good.

One particular morning, still in the spirit of reorganizing, I decided to take my floor-length mink coat, which I had bought when I was flush with money back in 1990, sneak it into my car, and drive it up to the consignment shop about ten miles away.

Boy, it felt good to drive again.

When I shoved the heavy coat over the counter for their forthcoming autumn collection, the woman said, "We aren't taking those until after Labor Day."

I was starting to lose energy by that time.

I knew I was being manipulative, but I said, "I won't be returning with this. I just had breast surgery."

To my surprise, she said that she herself had had the same procedure two years before. Then she went on to tell me how she got septicemia, and her inserts fell out. The other woman behind the counter said, "I had my double mastectomy with reconstruction at Kaiser in the East Bay, and they forgot to put back my nipple. I sued them, but I lost."

I told them the brief version of my story.

"What are you doing carrying a heavy coat like this after only two weeks of recovery?"

I realized then that I wasn't just in the slow lane. I was in a ditch, and I better damn well learn to like it. I was a lucky dog so far, compared to what I had just heard, but I was tempting fate. I got back in my car and went home, jumped into bed, and started watching trashy television: *Hoarders, Storage Wars,* and *Snapped.* I gave thanks that I was cancer free and accepting my life in the slow lane.

Now at Maui Memorial, I was yet again in the slow lane, and the outcome was uncertain.

I was in a hospital. It was like one of those reoccurring landscapes in dreamlife—landscapes that are instantly familiar because you've been there before. It was part of the dream-repertoire-landscape-sequence embedded in the brain. The endless branching corridors and circular nurses' station all looked identical. And then there were those innocuous paintings—still lifes of flowers or landscapes that seemed to have been specifically chosen to leave no impression. There were doorways through which you occasionally saw a bunch of Mylar balloons or a pair of pale, withered legs. The nurses no longer wore white hose, with pert little white caps on their heads. They were in scrubs printed in patterns that were relentlessly cheerful: prints with hearts, teddy bears, sunflowers, or peace signs. The air was still and stifled and the smell of hospitals was like ladies' rooms in large department stores: there was a pleasant chemical odor, but you knew that its function was to hide something. Time moved differently in hospitals than in the outside world—both slower and faster. Minutes stood still, but the hours evaporated. The day was long and less structured, measured only by meals on trays and the taking of vital signs, the changing of IV bags, medication schedules, occasional tests, and trips to the bathroom along with the attached rolling IV gizmo.

I was panicking. What if I couldn't find my doctor, and no one answered my nurse's call button? My leg—was it gone? How did this happen when I didn't feel anything? Did they take my leg while I was napping? Why didn't they tell me first before they took it?

17. Remembering the Death of a Friend

THERE WERE WARNING SIGNS before the shark attack, but I was utterly unprepared for what happened.

Without being aware of it, I had used my parents as a reassuring model of how they sailed through their fifties to their end zone. They acquired more stuff, seemed to get more relaxed with age, remodeled the kitchen, took a cruise to Aruba, and enjoyed the money they had tirelessly saved.

I thought of this as I lay in Maui Memorial Hospital, wishing I could call my mother. I silently compared our lives. It was only after she died that I began to see her as a woman with unfulfilled needs and wants, as more than just my mother.

I remembered how I was looking through the cartons in the attic after she died when I came across a shoebox. It was tied up in a grosgrain ribbon popular decades ago. In the box lay love letters from my dad, but near the bottom were some romantic postcards and airmail letters from someone who loved her and signed, "Your secret admirer."

I couldn't imagine my mother having a life as a young woman. What could she have told me about that? What kind of woman was she before and after she took on the opaque role of my mother?

I went back in my mind, trying to access what she had been doing at age sixty-three. I was living in Cambridge with my second husband and just gotten my doctorate. I'd moved from California to live and work in Massachusetts, and yet I only saw my parents twice a year, even though I lived only two hours away. Why did I keep them at such an emotional distance? Could I have broken through and made a connection with the woman inside my mom?

Before my parents began to fail physically, my mom took on the task of cleaning out the attic and the basement because she didn't want to leave anything for us to have to deal with after she died. Each time I called or visited, she showed me her progress. Wasn't she too busy thinking at that time about aging and dying to take on this task? She often gave me instructions such as, "When I die, don't forget to stay in touch with your brother. And remember not to go to bed angry with your husband." I could never even imagine my mother aging, much less dying. She had boundless energy, boundless enthusiasm, and even boundless judgments.

"But Mom, you are getting so good at throwing things out. I can imagine you and Dad sitting on top of one or two suitcases on the side of the curb, waiting for the grim reaper to arrive." We both thought that was very funny. In our family, dark humor was the only kind of humor to have, besides blatant cynicism.

Hadn't I seen the warning signs before the shark attack? They were right in front of me all the time, like red flags bobbing on buoys floating ahead of me in the water, indicating that something was going on beneath the surface.

And just like with the passing of my mother and father, so it was with my longtime friend Ava. In early May of 1989, when Ron and I began going to Maui, Ava happened to be vacationing several miles away from us in a high-rise condo on the beach. She called me and asked if she could go snorkeling with me to find the turtles.

The next morning, I met her at our rented place in Makena and entered the water down a rocky path nearby. We swam out several hundreds of yards and headed to where I had marked off in my mind the intersection of the red roof of a stucco house and the biggest palm tree closest to the water — an organic marker of longitude and latitude.

If we looked down from where we floated fourteen feet above, we could see turtles the size of small Volkswagens docked against the soft surface that green, abundant algae afforded. In what other part of the world could we be part of such a scene? It always took my breath away. Ava and I felt the sacredness of what we were allowed to view. I can only say "allowed" because the scene was something few people knew about — my own private rock.

Ava turned to me and said, "Did I ever tell you that I have epilepsy?"

"No," I said. Some breath went out of me. "Why are you telling me here?"

"Well, I felt no need to, but when I get stressed, I feel it coming on."

"Is it coming on now?"

"Well, no — but I thought I ought to tell you, just in case."

"Ava, what would you want me to do? I don't know CPR."

"Well, get me back to the beach, I guess."

On the outside I tried to appear calm, but my mind raced as I started to edge back the way we came. The only CPR I had learned was breathing into a plastic doll's mouth several years before in a day-long training. I cut our adventure short and made sure we drifted back to shore without lingering. Ava chatted while inanely smiling the whole time, not understanding how she had put us in potential danger. What if she had had a seizure in the water? I was both angry at her in a childish way for ruining our outing and confused that after twenty years of friendship, she hadn't disclosed before now that she had had epilepsy all her life. I loved her creativity and intelligence. Besides, she was always ready for something new. We had so many playful times together.

Back on the shore, she said, "The strangest thing happened this morning. I found myself driving the wrong way down South Kihei Road. I couldn't understand why cars were honking at me. Oh, I'm so angry with myself. How could I do such a thing?"

The next day, the phone rang at eight o'clock in the morning. "Who calls on a vacation at that hour?" Ron whispered as he handed me the phone. It was Ava.

"Hi. I'm in the hospital," she said lightly, "I was taken here last night. I was diagnosed with a brain tumor."

Ava died in surgery a few days later. She was younger than me. They flew her body back to the mainland. I went to her cremation at nine in the morning at Fernwood Cemetery on Tennessee Valley Road in Mill Valley several weeks later.

Fernwood had been a pet cemetery, from what I remembered. Now they had taken on humans — funerals and cremations. It was a beautiful spot, only a forty-five minute walk from the trailhead to the ocean in Southern Marin.

The morning of Ava's service, I was so preoccupied with thoughts about her that I missed the turnoff and sat in traffic mindlessly watching kids from the Mill Valley Middle School swarm past me in the crosswalk with their backpacks, skateboards, and baggy clothes. We called it junior high back when I was in school. The whole system had changed since I was that age. I tried to remember what I had worn in junior high as I waited for the light to change. Suddenly, I realized that I was headed for the Golden Gate Bridge. Once again, I turned around.

I was filled with small, petty, and mean-spirited thoughts as I got the car back on track. I was thinking about Ava's obituary in *The Chronicle*. I'd read it online to Ron. Who wrote this? It didn't represent Ava's richly textured life and accomplishments at all. All it talked about was her deceased husband's notoriety, and how Ava was his helpmate.

I was brooding over that when I entered Fernwood's cold stone and floor-to-ceiling, windowed interior that was nestled against a gray rock hill.

The Buddhists talk about dying. And all the usual Buddhist suspects were at the funeral. Large celebrity egos, wannabe egos, and small, follower egos.

The brief Buddhist ceremony took only forty-five minutes from start to finish. The ceremony was pristine and sparsely worded, with lots of bowing. I had done my time, like any other New Age person at the Zen Center, and logged in workshops and all-day retreats, but I felt gypped on this particular morning. It seemed like there was no there, there.

I became a bit despairing. If reality was an illusion, was there only impermanence and uncertainty? Let me have someone to project upon, I thought. Don't spoil my childlike innocence with Buddhists' emptiness and impermanence.

The thirty of us all rose and walked down long corridors behind the Buddhist abbot as her lay priests echoed our chant: "May Ava be at peace."

We entered a chamber that looked like a boiler room that echoed with compressors and high whining sounds that chugged and stopped periodically. Some members of the party shouldered the coffin containing the occupant, Ava. A metal oven automatically opened.

Ava was swiftly tossed in, like a pizza thrown into the oven. Then the thought evaporated, and a chill went through me.

As Ava was being cremated, I asked her this to elevate her spirit: "Please come to me in my dreams. Let me know what it's like. Don't just do the movie-thing and tell me you're okay. Let me know—do they have cronuts, a Wednesday night movie, can you swim or play scrabble? Does God really look like Charlton Heston? Be specific, please."

Later, I felt angry at Ava as I lay in bed waiting for sleep. I thought she would meet me in my dream life like my mom and dad had after they died. I wanted her to come and tell me she was safe now, but there were no dreams with Ava in them.

Several weeks after the cremation, I got a call from Ava's stepdaughter. She asked me to go to Ava's house and look through her computer, albums, and boxes of slides and put together a slideshow for her forthcoming memorial service at a local congregational church. The house key was under the Buddha statue inside the gate in the back yard.

The Northern California day was overcast. The house was an old Victorian in Mill Valley. The shades were drawn as I looked up at the second floor where her study was located. The leaded windows that looked like impersonal eyes reflected the gray day.

I steeled myself, not liking to walk into an uninhabited house. I walked from room to room, looking for her stuff. It seemed as though many people had been through the house already. There were piles and piles of furniture, clothes, and dishes — all the stuff that makes up a life — swept into the middle of the elegant dining room, living room, and study. Upstairs, the carpets had been pulled up and papers, files, and cardboard boxes of photos were stacked — to be carted away, I supposed.

I went into her study and found boxes and boxes of her fiber, three-dimensional artwork dumped onto the middle of the floor. I bent down and began putting them into grocery bags and hauling them to my car.

I remember her art installations when she rented a storefront and had one of her many art openings. We critiqued each other's work. She was instrumental in visioning and remodeling our local art gallery, and working in her own art studio out back of her home, but she was so much more than that.

So, this is what happens in the end. I'd always lived with the conviction that it never could happen to me. Like a cork, I bounced up to the surface again, from the depths of life into the world of denial. I didn't heed the warning.

18. Dread & Marriage Theory

THERE WAS ANOTHER WARNING SIGN before the shark attack. This time, I caught myself measuring every moment of joy as if it would never return: admiring my niece's smooth skin as she got off the Marin Airporter with a bouncy step, laughing with a neighbor over our failed flower garden eaten by deer, or dancing in the living room with Ron to Ivan Lin's Brazilian music, which played in the background. Was it that long ago that each moment of joy was taken for granted because we knew there would be many more? I hadn't even thought about how time was slipping away. Nieces grew up, neighbors moved, and Ron was waning in energy as we flew around the living room to the music. When did my recognition of the passing of time start to change? It was slow and imperceptible in recognizing that these moments of joy might never return.

At first, our growing old together was humorous, and we both laughed at it. Ron and I were standing on the upper landing outside our house with a construction guy negotiating a new roof. The old roof was leaking through the skylights and the front ceiling. The contractor gave us a price for a twenty, thirty, and forty-year roof.

"Which one do you want to go with?" he asked.

Ron and I looked at each other. It was as though the same thought crossed our minds simultaneously. "We'll take the twenty year one," Ron said. We were sixty. We wouldn't be in this house long enough to see the demise of a twenty-year roof. It seemed very funny to us at the time. We took the twenty year one.

Over time, I developed a theory about relationships, using my own experiences and my husband's as a research project and a longitudinal study. I called it marriage, version 3.0 because I had been married twice before, so I felt an ironic sense of mastery.

My marriage theory started with the first stage, which was initiated by testosterone and estrogen poisoning—The Romantic Phase. The When-Harry-Met-Sally Phase of the relationship. It was characterized by love, lust, and sex. Many movies and made-for-television series were about this romantic stage: from *Annie Hall, Sex in the City,* or twisted love like *Fatal Attraction.* My husband called *Fatal Attraction* a training film. Most couples went their own way after this stage fizzled, but many moved on to the next phase.

It was The Death Spiral. Women called it: The Where-is-This-Relationship-Going, Phase? At this point, the conversation was led by the women and went something like this:

"Let's get married. I can't waste my childbearing years being in limbo with you."

"Mmm," he would say. "Can I think about it and do it for homework?"

"No. We've been together for two years. You love me, right?"

"Right."

"Say it, then,"

"Err, do I have to? Okay. I love you."

"Then why don't you want to get married?"

After a long pause, he would say, "Because I was married once before and I'm afraid of going through the same thing again."

She would say, "Don't you feel guilty for wasting two years of my life? Look, you have several choices. You can either marry me, or we can chalk this up to a Marin growth experience and I will move far away where you'll never hear from me or see me again, and I'll take all my furniture and the cat—or I can kill you. Now, which do you choose? Decide now!"

"Okay. Let's get married."

The reasoning went like this for him: If two years of romance were good, twenty years would be even more fun: steady sex. Since a myriad of men had gone before him, and they had endured, so could he.

Fast forward to six months after the wedding. The thought had occurred to her—the woman—at three in the morning that she had made an awful mistake: she had married the wrong man. Not that the right one was ever waiting in the wings, but what emerged was what I called The Buyer's Remorse Phase. And like the commercials you saw on television, this little black cloud was often hanging over the whole relationship.

The marriage soon triggered what I'd observed as The Modern-Family-Phase: each spouse busy helping the other with career advice, childrearing problems, and saving money to buy a house. This phase could endure for as long as thirty years. The sex became less frequent, but they both focused on the kids. In fact, when they went on exotic vacations to Europe, or a cruise to Bermuda, they mostly talked about the kids.

The next phase began organically when menopause sneaked up on the woman, or the man came home with a red Corvette. That's when buyer's remorse reared up again. The woman would begin to feel like she had been slowly and unwittingly subjugated for the last thirty years, losing herself, compromising, and not being able to find herself amidst the kids' and her husband's needs. Her husband would find her increasingly bitchy and cranky. I called it The Stockholm-Syndrome Phase—loving your captor-husband or wife. On the other hand, the husband had decided he liked his couch, his television, his hot shower, and his thirty years of room service. He was happy and settled in. He still hadn't figured out what the room with the refrigerator was.

She would go into therapy, take a yoga course, fall in lust with her personal trainer, and realize that there was no one out there who would tolerate having sex with her in a well-lit room. It was too late for a face-lift and too early for the nursing home. She would realize her husband was too old for her to control, and too young to die.

This propelled us into the last and final phase that I called The Until-Death-Do-Us-Part Phase. The couple finally settled into a relaxed and contented last phase—the end zone. They respected each other's routines: he snored. She flossed vigorously in bed. When they sensed a fight was brewing, over the years they had developed a code. For example: my husband's code was, "We're headed towards *Fucksville.*" *Fucksville* was a small imaginary town in the Midwest with a decimal point as a zip code, one gas station, and a huge city dump. You could smell the foul air for miles around. You didn't want to be in *Fucksville.* Sometimes, I'd say, "We are five miles away. Oops, we are two miles away."

"I think we just parachuted into *Fucksville,*" Ron would say. We didn't know that we had triggered one another and were headed into some rocky terrain.

The couple would joke about dying. He would say, "I want to die in my sleep." She would say, "Let me know the night before and I'll sleep in the guest room. I don't want to wake up to a blue man."

She would say, "The day after I die, there will be gridlock on our street with women in cars bringing you casseroles."

He would say, "You'll have this place remodeled in a week. The day after I die, there will be gridlock on this street with contractors and painters. They're probably on speed dial right now." And up popped buyer's remorse again.

However, this was also the stage of deep friendship and custodial duties. When she wanted some ice cream at ten in the evening, like an old buddy, he drove to the 7-Eleven.

I knew we were entering a new stage when Ron was asked by an impressionable, twenty-something couple that was deeply in love, "What is the secret of your long marital success?"

My husband paused, looked over his shoulder to see if I was nearby, and whispered, "Fatigue."

We were somewhere between The Stockholm-Syndrome Phase and The Until-Death-Do-Us-Part Phase one year before the shark tragedy struck.

We were in Maui, taking a mid-morning walk on the beach. It was an ordinary day in paradise: flat blue sky and the surf rolling up and back licking our toes. The island was welcoming the warmth of the day, with rising humidity. Maui had no edges: it was all sun, surf, and embracing air. Softness pervaded everything. We were baking in the middle of the ocean. The Hawaiian Islands are two hundred and twenty-five hundred miles away from the nearest landmass.

Then we hopped in the car to go to the health food store, where Ron bought his latest elixir—a shake of orange juice, a banana, garlic, and two cloves. "An old Hawaiian wisdom potion," his friend Jake had told us.

I waited in the car outside the store. A young man with Rastafarian dreadlocks strummed on his ukulele, and another man smoked a cigarette while slurping on a green drink. A woman walked by with a rooster on her shoulder and then disappeared into the store. The humidity was slowing everyone's brain. The humidity made us walk around in various states of undress. Men went bare chested into the market, and women wore loose fitting, thin sundresses with nothing on underneath. Everyone wore flip-flops. It was the bed-head look of fashion.

Later, in the humid afternoon, as we lay on the couch in the condo and watched CNN on television, the latest bad news felt disconnected from our life on Maui, like a tale from some other world. On the islands, you might as well be living on another planet. But trouble found us: Ron said, "I don't feel good. I've got to lie down—I feel like the lights are going out." I thought it had been caused by the drink from the health food store.

He looked gray and clammy. I acted on instinct. I couldn't take a chance. I grabbed his shirt, got him into the car, and drove to Urgent Care, a building we'd only noticed recently on nearby Lipoa Street. When we arrived, the office seemed empty. The doctor, a sour and serious-looking man, took Ron's EKG.

"It's abnormal," the doctor said.

"Could it be food poisoning?" I asked.

"No, it doesn't present that way."

The doctor left the room. Ron and I joked about his demeanor: pale like a vampire, with dark, long pauses in his speech. I remember saying jokingly, "He needs some sun."

"He looks like Dracula," I remember Ron saying.

Even then, we were ready to hop in the car, with the relief of a diagnosis behind us, and head toward the beach despite Ron's gray and clammy face and diminishing energy.

The doctor returned to the room and said, "Ron needs to go to Maui Memorial by transport—an ambulance ride." Ron and I looked at each other in shock. I remember Ron saying, "Can't we just drive there?"

"No—this is no laughing matter. You may be having a heart attack or a stroke."

Moments later, I met the ambulance driver in the parking lot outside of Urgent Care and drove the rental car behind the blaring sirens on a perfectly cloudless beach day on the Pilani Highway to Maalea Harbor and past the golf course to Wailuku and the Maui Hospital emergency room. I was upset and annoyed that our vacation day was ruined.

My car radio announced, "Temperatures will be in the high nineties with eighty-five percent humidity. Here's a blast from the past, for your listening pleasure." The Rolling Stones came on next with "Wild Horses."

When we got to the emergency room, the doctor asked me to go back to the condo and get all the drugs that Ron had been taking before this episode, since neither of us could name the drugs and the exact dosage when interviewed on intake. Quickly, I left Ron and drove right into gridlock on the two-lane highway. Twenty minutes before, there had been an accident. I followed a long line of cars weaving in and out of strange neighborhoods, trying to find a shortcut to get out of the traffic on Pilani Highway. The houses looked like they were made from toothpicks and toilet paper, built the night before. Each house in the subdivision had a postage-stamp size lawn and a newly laid sidewalk. I kept ending up in one cul de sac after another. It was maddening. It felt like a workday on the mainland. Finally, back at the condo, I pillaged through his suitcase and drawers to find his medications to bring back to the hospital. Maybe there had been a drug interaction that the doctors could fix and make him right again. In my mind, I was still seeing us on the beach by noon.

When I got back, Ron was out of his mind with fear. Behind my façade of keeping it together I, too, was unraveling inside. I kept sighing and silently nagging myself, "When can we go back to the beach? What will I do without him? This can't be happening."

In the earlier stages of our marriage, we thought we were so independent, and not at all enmeshed like our parents were: we had separate bank accounts, separate sets of friends, and — at times — separate travel plans. We weren't going to live our parents' lives. I secretly thought that we could walk away from the marriage any time. Over time, we saw each other through our parents' deaths, his brother's divorce, operations, and with no children — by design — it was easy to be selfish.

When I think of having a baby, I imagine going shopping with my sleeping infant in a stroller, and a dress catches my eye. I'm engrossed, walk into the fitting room to try it on, and realize I could get it at Target for half the price, fly out of the store, hop into my car, and drive across town to Target, completely forgetting about the sleeping baby I'd left behind.

Children felt like an awesome responsibility after my anxious childhood. But now there was no kid to call. Friends weren't obligated. They could walk away from us any time. Besides, I hadn't had time to cultivate friends. I cultivated my career.

Once, when we had to drag an old washing machine down three flights of stairs, I complained to Ron, "If we had had a son, we could have called him to carry it down free of charge." I envisioned a handsome twenty-four-year old with broad shoulders who was completely dedicated to us.

Ron countered with, "If we had a son, it would have cost us about three hundred thousand dollars to feed, clothe him, and put him through school. We can call a guy with a truck to haul it away for fifty bucks."

As night approached, they sedated Ron and asked me to leave the hospital. Back at the condo, I felt a great sense of loneliness mixed with the strangeness of Ron not sleeping beside me. When was the last time we had slept apart? I couldn't remember. Images of going back to the empty house after my mother died in St. Barnabas Hospital clicked continuously like color snapshots in my mind.

I kept thinking about how Ron had seemed to be feeling tired, which was why we had planned a vacation. I nagged at myself, asking if there was anything I could have done or could do now to make this situation better. Finally, after two episodes of *Law & Order* and two glasses of wine, I fell into a troubled sleep.

That night a reoccurring dream, but this time I couldn't find my way to Ron's hospital room. All night long, I wandered, lost, down the hospital corridors.

As I drove back to the hospital the next morning, hungover from the restless night before, I recalled one of our early dates. On a clear, cold, starry night, I anticipated entering my apartment alone. I turned to him. "I hate Sunday nights. They always remind me of endings, and they make me feel lonely."

"You are not alone any more. We have each other." I knew then that I had found my soulmate.

19. Heart Surgery

THAT MORNING, I CALLED JAKE from Ron's hospital room. He came right away. He sat at Ron's bedside and talked to Ron about the immediate future. Cowed by the situation, I left to sign papers put in front of me at the patient coordinator's office. I didn't know what I was signing, but in the back of my mind it represented forward movement. Yet it reminded me so much of the last days with my mom that terror filled my belly.

So far they couldn't find out what was wrong, but Ron was failing. I felt like I was in a wash and spin cycle.

He needed a cardiogram, but there was no cardiac surgeon on the island. If there were an unforeseen problem in this procedure, there would be no backup. Dr. Schwab, the closest cardiac surgeon, couldn't immediately get to Maui from Honolulu.

This wasn't the first time we had had a close call concerning Ron's heart. We were in Mill Valley last time. I remembered calling 911 several years back when Ron woke me at three in the morning to tell me he was having a heart attack. The firemen and the police squad car came within five minutes. The fire truck hissed and belched as it rumbled up our driveway, breaking the silence of our remote, forested neighborhood.

The firemen stomped in with intensity and urgency. They were big, hulking young guys ready for action. I thought of asking them to remove their boots; I didn't want them to ruin our carpets. Then I thought it was best not to say anything, because if Ron died, I'd probably be a suspect. My mind was muddled.

Meanwhile, Dr. Schwab conferred with Dr. Wexman, Ron's doctor back home. They decided to do a nuclear heart scan first. Ron was transported to the basement of the building, and all afternoon he went through tests. Each test result was ominous, yet there was no diagnosis. Our friends from the island, Natalie and Wes, sat struggling through small talk while we awaited the results and ate hospital-made sandwiches: tuna with mayo on white bread. The basement was windowless. It smelled of antiseptic. Every so often, a woman would come by with a cart filled with cleaning supplies and wipe down a new part of the corridor. She seemed to be working her way to the reception area. She had probably seen so many like us before. We were invisible. Even then, we talked about being back on the beach by four after Ron had aced every test.

At three fifty, the Maui doctor told us that Ron had a blockage, and had to be medically flown to Honolulu. The nurse and the doctors agreed that he and I could go together on the small plane that would meet the ambulance at the airport.

I sat by Ron's bedside. He wasn't talking. His skin was pale, and a gray pallor was spreading over his face. I was worried.

"Ron, do you think you can make it through the flight?"

No answer.

His forehead felt clammy and hot. Behind him, sighing and beeping, the machines delivered fluids and monitored his vital signs.

I was upset and done with this drama. I wanted to go home. I couldn't sit still. I roamed the hall looking for the doctor.

When I spotted him, I launched into my angst without any greeting.

"I'm worried that Ron won't get through the flight because he is getting so depressed and unresponsive."

I could feel the doctor tighten and then he paused, but before he could speak again, I jumped in.

"Can't we just fly him home?" I asked.

He cleared his throat and spent a second or two looking at me through rimless glasses. I felt like a small child insisting on my way.

"That would be foolhardy. He would have heart failure on the plane."

"But what if he doesn't make it?"

"If you insist, you can sign him out as unauthorized and proceed at your own risk."

He turned and walked away down the hall. I was left standing there in despair. I didn't want to sign Ron out unauthorized. He needed whatever help he could get.

I tried to reconstruct each moment. I was simply losing track of time. It was blurring. What was the sequence of events? How long did we spend in the emergency room? Exactly what were the names of the nurses and doctors who came in and out? How long did the tests take downstairs?

In my head, during Ron's crisis, I spent a great deal of time trying to keep track of time, trying to reconstruct each moment and the exact sequence of events that were unfolding. This has always been my go-to way of coping—this reconstruction with the names, telephone numbers, dates, and times of contact.

It helped me through the terror of my childhood and my anxious family. Ron called this kind of note taking and worry "Jewish meditation."

In my notes were: "9:00 a.m., Dobutamine Stress Echo-IV line with drug, Transesophogeal Ecohocardiogram (TEE) (A probe in the esophagus that produced sound waves to create images of his heart). 10:00 a.m., Stress Echo Sound Wave. Nothing conclusive. 11:00 a.m., Ron continues to fail. He looks almost gray and is only semi-conscious."

How could this happen when everything else was normal? The sun was out, and palm trees were swaying against the blue sky.

He lay there, gray and clammy, as the numbers on the monitor changed with small pings. I could not get those numbers straight, no matter which nurse I asked. I asked a different nurse each time, because I didn't want to appear stupid. I could not concentrate. Which one was the blood pressure, pulse, or heart rate?

"12:00. He has stopped talking."

If he could just get up off the bed, we could go back to the beach.

At Queen's Hospital in Honolulu he'd get a cardiogram and the surgery he needed. I ran back to the condo and packed a small bag for the island-hopping.

I arrived back just in time. A small plane was waiting to take him to Honolulu immediately. Three orderlies tried to heave him from the hospital sheets onto the gurney to take him downstairs, out the back door, and into an ambulance that was waiting on the tarmac outside the hospital. Drugged and screaming, he grabbed at things to take with him. Lunging at the water glass, a tissue box beside the bed, the comb on the table — he struggled as they tied him down to stop him flailing at the transporters.

Two beefy orderlies pushed him out the double metal doors. The doors slammed in my face. Ron was gone. Ron was in a thin patient gown, with no shoes or identification. How could he return to Maui if he had gone off into the world with no wallet and no shoes? I began sobbing.

Suddenly, a nurse pulled me aside.

"Change of plans. You can't go with him because the winds have come up, and there would be too much weight on the plane." She placed her hand on the small of my back, ignoring my sobs, and led me to the side door, shoving it open, holding it with her hip, pushing my roll-aboard bag ahead of me, and swiftly ushered me outside. She put my roll-aboard handle back in my hand. Our eyes did not meet. No words were exchanged. The door locked shut behind me.

I stood in the hospital parking lot alone. I heard an anguished sound come from my lips.

In a daze, I stood watching Ron be carted away in the distance. I was on the verge of losing it. The hot sun beat down on me. It was only twenty-four hours since our life together had taken an abrupt turn.

My back and feet had been hurting for hours. My lower back was cramping, and I felt tired and raw, but only now did I really begin to feel it. The sun was scorching. I walked to the main entrance reception area of the hospital, looking for some shade so I could think clearly. I could call someone—but who? Why wouldn't the buzzing in my head stop? On the inpatient form I signed, I had left the incase-of-emergency blank. Without Ron, no children, and no family close by, I had no one to call.

Over the years, when Ron had looked at me, I felt young and pretty. How could I live without that look if I didn't have him? Who else would ever have known me that way? How could time have gone by so fast? The last time I looked, we were forty and just buying our first house. After all these years, we'd never told each other how deep our feelings ran in the way that people do when they know they are losing one another—like you see in the movies. Ron and I had slowly become so enmeshed, just like our parents. We had changed imperceptibly over the years.

I first met him at a professional conference. I looked at him and thought, that is what a face of a kind man should look like—open, no deception. That is the face I would make if I were God. Dark curly hair, deep Paynes gray eyes, broad strokes for the jaw line with high cheekbones. I would love to paint that face.

How could I go on alone? He brought out the best in me, and we grew each other up. We had blinked, and time had landed us here. How could that be? If he were gone, there would be no one who knew the whole of our lives. I didn't even know the whole of it. Writing everything down in my journals felt like an exercise now to capture the moment when everything passed—and I would pass, too.

I had kept journals since I learned to write. My first journal was a small green diary with a lock and key that my mom gave me for my seventh birthday. Then came spiral bound notebooks, followed most recently by black and white marbled composition books. I kept them in a cabinet under the bookshelves upstairs in the hallway—an out of the way alcove where no one would look. I collaged the covers as I went along. The pages inside held my innermost secrets: my disappointments, perceived slights, desires, longing, insecurities, and jealousies. In writing, I discovered a way into myself. It was a place to write poison pen letters that I would never send. I wrote for sheer joy of feeling the black gel pen connect to the page. It helped me make sense out of my world — a way to gather myself, dig deep, discover what I thought and felt, revisit my younger selves, and reconnect. Reading excerpts back, I saw that as I got into my fifties, I was no longer critical of myself. I was compassionate about my younger self that was in so much pain over everyday things. Back then, the world had moved too slowly for me. I anticipated with worry things that never actually happened. I imagined far more catastrophes in my head that could have happened, but didn't. I poured out my soul.

The process felt magical. In contrast, the world offered no explanation.

The belief that no one would help me — nor was I the kind of person that could ask for help — had been embedded deep inside me as a child. As a child, I'd learned that both the world and the people you trusted could be flawed and cruel. Don't ask for anything — because you'll be disappointed, I had learned. Now with Ron gone, I was desperate.

I got out my cell phone and started dialing frantically: people I knew on Maui. Hoping for what? Reassurance, grounding, or some reasonable advice? I got several answering machines, and then I reached a live person — Jake. He offered something I'd never expected from him — or from any other human being.

"I'll come get you and we'll go to Honolulu together."

Like a professional traveler, Jake led me through the Kahului Airport maze to a commercial flight to Honolulu, hailed a taxi at the arrival gate, handed me to the nurse at the admitting area at Queen's Hospital in Honolulu, and finally led me to the hospital housing that Maui Memorial had arranged for us.

At Queen's Hospital, Ron's cardiogram showed that he had a left bundle branch block. The operation would be a ligation of the right coronary artery to the main pulmonary artery fistula and a ligation of the diagonal coronary artery to the main pulmonary artery fistula.

"It was not a heart attack," the doctor said, "but a congenital condition that should have been spotted early in life. It's the kind of condition you hear about when a young athlete suddenly drops dead on the basketball court." It explained Ron's usual upbeat energy followed by a sudden lack in stamina.

His surgeon, Dr. Dang, took Jake and me behind the scenes and showed us an image of the cardiogram, and told us what he was going to do. Then he sat on Ron's bed and explained the procedure to him. Even in Honolulu, I had a shred of hope that Ron would simply recover. I kept wishing that Ron would get up out of bed, refuse surgery, walk out of there with me, take a flight back to Maui, and finish the day on the beach.

My mind was muddled. Ron needed to give Dr. Dang permission to go ahead with the surgery to ligate the fistula in a three-hour operation with uncertain results. When we left Ron that evening, he was drugged and in shock, and he still hadn't decided to go ahead with surgery. The situation was wearing on us.

That night, to take our mind off things, Jake took me out to dinner at a restaurant in Chinatown. I gulped down a glass of white wine, ordered a rack of lamb and ate it quickly, then ordered another glass of wine. We talked about cars, prices of cars, and colors of cars. We did an inventory of all the cars we used to own. I did not know how I was going to get through the evening and what was in store for the next day. When we got back to the hospital compound, we wandered around looking for the housing they had provided for us.

Finally, we found the apartment in a complex of huge, pre-war buildings that sprawled for blocks in downtown Honolulu and adjacent to the hospital. Inside, it was a dark, dirty, cavernous structure. I could sense that it was built for large families with little money who were awaiting news and who were in limbo — just like we were. Broken furniture sat in the corner of rooms and the toilet didn't flush. We both crashed in different rooms under the grinding noise of a window air conditioner, but oblivious to our surroundings. I slept like a rock.

When we arrived at Ron's bedside the next morning, he told us that he had decided during the night to have surgery that morning. He said weakly, "I'm tired of feeling so awful."

The morning of Thursday, May twenty-fifth, a year before my shark attack — almost to the day — Ron went through three hours of heart surgery.

As Ron was rolled into the operating room to be cut open, Jake jumped up and hurried me outside to a waiting taxi. Within seconds, he was the driver's best friend. The taxi driver waited while Jake booked me into the Hawaiian Prince Hotel on Waikiki — a Japanese, non-tourist hotel.

"You won't get the Bermuda-short set vibe here because you won't understand what most of the tourists are saying," Jake said jokingly as he negotiated the kama'aina rate for locals.

Then I learned the real reason Jake was eager to accompany me to Honolulu.

"Let's buy a Mini Cooper," he said. "No, I'm just kidding, but let's test drive one."

Then he made the taxi driver wait at a Mini Cooper dealership while he talked cars with the sales manager. Jake knew how to play, and I forgot everything for three hours. I forgot about Ron, my worries vanished, and I played at making believe we were buying a Mini Cooper for Jake.

When Ron came out of surgery, he had tubes going in all directions: one for breathing, one for urine, one for bowels, and one for oxygen. Immediately, Jake and I could see that Ron had gotten his color back.

"I've joined the zipper club," he said, with a wan smile as he showed us the seven-inch slash on his chest.

"You're back on planet Earth," said Jake.

The hollowness returned as I walked down to the main entrance of Queen's Hospital to say goodbye to Jake. He hailed a cab to the airport to catch a plane back to Maui as if we had been on a casual weekend date. Ron was in ICU, and still not out of the woods. I was alone again.

I reviewed a few facts: I was sixty-two. Ron was six weeks younger than me. He often teased me that I was a cougar. "You were the scout. Just like you to be so anxious that you popped out first to see if it was safe."

We had been married for twenty-four years. We had no children, five cats (in total, not at the same time). We had attended a dozen weddings, two bar mitzvahs, buried four parents, attended several memorial services. People in Marin generally don't bury their loved ones. (They are too ecologically conscious). We'd traveled to four states and eight countries together. We'd had more than our share of knock down and drag out arguments. We had railed against each other even while knowing that projection was a reflection of self—our own self-hatred hurled at one another. Our favorite joke was, "You can give me feedback, but don't get any on me." (Meaning—I only want praise and recognition, not bile-ridden words.)

Sometimes we got to the edge of the metaphorical cliff, and together looked down into the abyss below, and pulled back in horror. We clung to each other, fearing abandonment. We both had divorces under our belt.

I looked at a photo of Ron on my iPhone. It was taken in Paia. He was riding a horse on the beach. He was smiling into the camera in the late afternoon sun. He was my strong and in charge Ron. He was my Jewish cowboy. We had stopped later at a small hut on a dirt road and tied the horses up outside to a post, just like in the movies. The place seemed like it was out in the middle of nowhere, but the lights were on. We went in, and they served us pizza.

When we had come out of the hut, it was dark. I remember how the horses knew their way home on the dirt road. We couldn't see a thing in front of us, but the horses knew, and we trusted them.

Whom did I trust now?

As I walked back into the hospital without Jake, I thought about how earlier in the week, Ron and I had stood in the surf overlooking the West Maui Mountains that were in the distance. He had said, "I never told you how lucky I felt when you came into my life." We continued to stand silently in waist-high water, gazing toward the horizon. "This is more than enough for me to just be with you here."

The next morning, they moved him up to a recovery unit on the sixth floor. By this time, he was determined to blow into the breath machine and get out of bed to sit in the chair four times a day as the doctor advised.

How do you ever anticipate the slow and insidious stress that builds in a crisis like water that is slowly coming to a boil? Ron was to remain in the hospital for ten days of our month in Maui.

That evening, on an impulse, I ran out of the hospital and hailed a cab to go to the Ala Moana Shopping Center. The familiar fragrance of Macy's from the perfume counter greeted me and permeated the store. The department store was empty at that hour. The search for absent saleswomen reminded me of home. I bought some sexy black underwear, a two-piece bikini, and a spandex dress. I told myself that I was spending this money so that I could wash the clothes I was wearing. I never wore the sexy underwear, the bikini, or the short dress. I felt too old and too tired to look good for myself, or anyone else. Then I rushed back to the hospital and stayed with Ron until they kicked me out. On the way out of the building, I passed a large mirror in the corridor and momentarily glanced into it. What I saw was an old, gray-haired lady with no makeup, who was wearing sneakers. She was a stranger to me. Then I recognized myself. How does one normalize in the face of crisis?

⌒

As the hospital was closing that night, I took a cab back to the Hawaiian Prince Hotel and ordered a Caesar salad and onion soup from room service. Then I slept fitfully. Early morning noises woke me.

That was how the routine unfolded. It was a marathon, not a sprint to get Ron released from Queen's Hospital. During the day, while Ron slept, I wandered the labyrinth of hallways. Unlike most hospitals, it had a long history of royalty. Named after Queen Emma and King Kamehameha IV, and located in downtown Honolulu, it was built in 1859. At that time, the continued existence of the Hawaiian race was seriously threatened by the influx of disease brought to the islands by foreign visitors. A smallpox epidemic in 1853 that had killed thousands of the dwindling population had caused this hospital to be built.

The walls were rough stucco, and on them hung oversized photographs of the queen, the king, and the whole royal family. The halls had a musty smell and reminded me of a third world country—it was not the titanium-white painted walls and linoleum floor, metal and steel of most other hospitals. There was the homey feeling of the subtropics like in *Casablanca*, and wide rattan chairs and tables sat outside the hallways, elevators, and outside the buildings. Dark-skinned families gathered in groups in those areas: small children, fathers, mothers breastfeeding their babies, and wrinkled, toothless grandmothers—all clinging together for safety and support in the middle of a crisis.

I wondered how much of life was about waiting: I began to sense in those corridors that time was linear—a chronology of the past, present, and future—then there was soul time. Soul time was a quality that could not be measured. It came from the inside out. Part of getting acquainted with soul time was learning how to listen to the silence and recognizing the pauses, the gaps, the stops, the heartbeat, and the breaths.

Time seemed to mold us. It was so malleable. Sometimes it went missing. Sometimes I had to let go of it and float to be able to survive.

The hospital had a large, grassy drive-through out front with a huge kapok tree in the middle. The tree appeared as if it had come with the hospital because of the canopy of high, arching branches shading much of the lawn. Sometimes in the late afternoons, when the humidity was so high that breathing was effortful, I wrapped my arms around the tree trunk, feeling its strength, and hugged it. The tree was an anchor when it felt like there was little else to hold onto.

When I couldn't sit any longer by Ron's bedside, I went out and sat on the ground under the tree as the sun slanted low and cast long shadows on the grass. It crossed my mind that strangers would see an older woman sitting in the middle of an empty expanse in the middle of a bustling city and wonder if I was homeless: an old lady outside a hospital entrance. I might have cared before this crisis, but I didn't care anymore what strangers might think.

Kapok trees have seedpods that are oddly shaped, like large, brown boomerangs with indentations for the seeds, and it is said by the Hawaiians that the seeds were used for oil that would bring light. Sometimes I wandered around the tree, looking for the most perfect pods to bring back and show Ron. Alone in a strange city, where the humidity made everyone seem to move in slow motion, I couldn't hear the noises beyond my sanctuary under the kapok. On the city streets away from the hospital campus, taxis and buses hauled tourists to the volcano, the beach, or the shopping malls. I was apart from all that. I felt numb to the rest of the outside world.

Under that kapok tree, I longed to return to Maui with Ron. Under that kapok tree, I recalled when we had first arrived before the heart episode. We had unpacked our suitcases and strode to the beach. The sun was setting in a glorious red ball as only Maui sunsets can do. Mother Maui puts on a show every dusk for locals and tourists alike. There are few places that I've been in my travels where people stop and gaze out to the horizon and stand reverently for several minutes watching the fireball sink and the sky change its mood into darkness. Some say that if you stare at the sunset you will see a green flash of fire around the sun before it finally drops into the ocean. A silence pervades the beachgoers. It is a sacred moment.

I remembered the other kapok tree on Maui. It was the one where the father had vanished after leaving his wallet, watch, towel, shirt, and pants behind the tree. I couldn't get the story out of my mind from the previous year. It had more meaning to me now.

The kapok tree that we had passed on our walks on the beach jutted out from the sand at water's edge. When the rental agent told us the story, I could picture the father. He was tired, having worked a long day, and thought a swim would invigorate him. He would have had a stocky build and been of medium height. He was the kind of man who had done hard physical labor earlier in his life, but now had a desk job in some small company, thanks to his son-in-law serving tourists on that congested island. I saw his wide, caramel-colored face with a strong jaw. And I felt his relief as the cool, saltwater wave first hit his body as he swam out farther. And then he disappeared. He simply went to the edge of this reality and crossed over to another place.

Was this an early warning to me one year before Ron's heart attack and two years before my shark attack? This could have been a prescient moment, or just another sad story. Who was to know that in the following May, almost to the day of Ron's heart failure, I would have my own encounter with the mysteries of Mother Maui?

Under the tree outside of Queen's Hospital, I thought that I could buy an airplane ticket and fly away. I could just disappear as if nothing had happened.

I had so many muddled thoughts. How did one find relief in times of crisis? Ron always teased me when I said that he was my best girlfriend. He said I taught him how to laugh. Now he was lying up on the fourth floor. There was nothing I could do but wait.

Joan Didion said, "A single person is missing for you and the whole world is empty." I walked around with a hole deep inside my stomach. Nothing made sense outside of this one focus. I only wanted to get him well and go back to Maui.

Later we learned that if this had happened in Marin, he would have survived without drama. He would have been ambulanced to UCSF and had a regular procedure followed by recovery at home, but we were in a third world country of sorts.

I recognized this when I made a call on the hospital phone to California. The mainland operator wanted to know the exchange from whatever overseas country I was calling from. I had to ask her where she went to school and why she didn't know that Hawaii was a state in the United States.

By the end of the week, after I had watched Ron walk around the ICU with a rolling IV stand that housed all his lactate ringer bags full of fluids, blow into a plastic tube, and take handfuls of medications around the clock, he was finally released.

By that time, many of the taxi drivers in Honolulu knew me, and the driver wished us luck when he dropped us off at the hotel. The contrast between the unrelenting sun and blue sky and the grimness of the long recovery ahead for my husband made me feel cranky. The external didn't reflect my internal state, and Ron was numb, stubborn, and angry that he wasn't in control of his fate. Angry that he had been blindsided, and that his body had betrayed him.

After his release, at the first sunset back at the hotel, after Ron got comfortable in bed, I turned on the television. I was surprised that so much time had passed and we were still in Honolulu. It was the weekend of Memorial Day, and the town was preparing for a Memorial Day eve celebration and the 65th anniversary of people who gave their lives in the service of their country. In real time, right outside our hotel, I saw exactly what the commentator on television was describing. The cameras panned the crowds of people assembled to the left of us in the Ala Moana Beach Park, right below our window.

I roused Ron, but he didn't have the strength to lift himself up to look.

"You gotta see this!" I shouted.

As the sun descended into the ocean, floating candles in paper lanterns in handmade little wood boats were sent off into the water. These specially-crafted floating lanterns — inscribed by hand with prayers and personal messages upon pieces of special paper affixed to each — were, after a beautiful ceremony of remembrance, launched lovingly into the water. It was a touching show of symbolism.

It felt so romantic to be a part of this ceremony. I wanted Ron to join me in my enthusiasm, and I wanted him to feel what I was feeling; but the irony was that we were actors in another reality that evening.

The ceremony itself celebrated honor and reverence for all life — and specifically served to pay homage to those veterans who so selflessly gave of their own lives so that we might enjoy the safety and freedoms of today. We listened to the opening sounds of the iconic Hawaiian shell trumpet, or *kani pū*, followed by Japanese taiko, the ceremony involved a chant, or *oli*, which called to six large parent lanterns offering prayers and gratitude. More and more lanterns were placed into the sea, and I thought about how the patient, repetitive pattern was the epitome of local Hawaiian culture, showcasing how protocol, and a code of etiquette was also revered and honored here. And although following such a prescribed protocol may have meant things moved more slowly — even appearing redundant — the purpose behind these practices was honor. We had seen similar protocol in the Hawaiian hula, in the presenting of lei and flowers, in the giving of blessings, in the simple pause between the bell ringing, and even in the hospital.

Now I understood the profound meaning behind the ceremony, as Honolulu residents gathered to pause, to honor, and to remember those who had passed, and to celebrate the amazing opportunity we had to be at peace with those around us — through the connective and unifying spirit of aloha. This ceremony seemed like an affirmation of both life and death in our lives. I looked at Ron and knew we were halfway to healing.

20. Coping

IT HAD BEEN SEVERAL DAYS since the shark attack. As I spent each day in an all-encompassing fog, time moved slower at this end of the hospital corridor. Toward the end of the first week, the incessant interruptions, and the excitement about a real live shark victim, seemed to have lessened. No doctors came by, less and less frequently a nurse came in to check on my meds, the lactate ringer bags — and me, the patient. The nurses were young, shy, and not very talkative. I was the stranger and the white person at the end of the hall. The novelty was gone.

When I closed my eyes, I imagined I was in a boat on the River Styx. Charon, a dark-cloaked ferry man standing up in his boat and pushing the water with his pole, was like a shadow hovering near the back of my mind. This healing thing was unpredictable. I might have passed the critical mark of life and death, or not. There were always changeups. Was I now into the part of my healing where there could be smooth sailing, or could a sudden rogue wave undo all the recovery so far? My healing could take a turn, and infection was my number one fear.

This image of Charon, the ferry man, was prescient as I thought of all the earlier moments when I had been painting abstract pictures of watery underworlds with predators, or remembering a past moment in Maui, driving a rental convertible and overcome with a lightheaded feeling that my life was about to change drastically.

On the fourth morning of my stay, an Asian nurse, bigger boned than the rest, entered the room. She brought in a pan filled with packets of towels that smelled of chemicals, but the smell was a clean fragrance like Bounce, Febreze or Lysol. She bent over me,

"May I give you a bath?"

"Yes."

I realized that I had been lying in the bed for days. Why didn't it occur to me to ask for a bath or a shower? I had gotten out of the bed to use the bathroom several times a day, but hadn't washed. In my vulnerability, I wondered if they had drawn straws for this dreary bath duty. My shark drama must have been an old story by now, as other patients arrived at the hospital with conditions more dire than mine. I had seen the nurses rushing past my door and heard the voice that communicated urgently through the loudspeaker several times a day.

"May I wash your feet?" she asked respectfully. I said, yes, thank you.

She tore open one plastic packet and methodically wiped first my right foot and then my left foot.

She stood up and took another packet from the pan.

"May I wipe your legs?" she asked.

"Yes," I said.

The wipes felt cool to my skin and refreshing, but I was wondering about the nurse's behavior. Two competing thoughts filled my mind. This behavior felt odd. In hospitals on the mainland, a nurse would be invasive, brusque, even impatient at times. I might feel like a commodity, and that this was a transaction. Was this nurse's behavior because I, as a white person in a culture of Asian people, was an outsider whom protocol would dictate you treat with respect, or was I the one visited by the Kahuna, the Maui wise man, and thus had earned respect? Or was I an anomaly in their world of patients—strange, foreign, and my behaviors just as puzzling to them as theirs were to me: a woman with people bringing me fins, with no family or kids surrounding my bedside day and night? Yelling on the phone to mainland television and radio producers? Was everyone treated this way? I was to never find out because—like so many other times in life—other things distracted me and intervened.

In the end, this was not the best bath I ever had. I can still feel the dry, powdery shampoo she used to wash my hair. In fact, it was hardly a wash, but more like trying to treat my cat with dry flea powder.

Finally I decided that just maybe I was an oddity to her and the rest of the nurses who worked there. They didn't know how to relate to me outside of their role, nor I them. After four days, I still couldn't get them, their names, or their faces straight in my head. Maybe it was because they all came and went, shift after shift. They all seemed slight, with light skin, and dark hair and eyes. As they all came and went, and multiplied day after day, they all began looking like the same person. I'd strike up a conversation with one, we'd have some vulnerable exchanges, and then I'd never see her again. I gave up trying to remember their names.

But what was heartening to me as I regained my strength were all the calls and visits from friends I didn't even know I had. Milo's wife, who had massaged me numerous times during our many visits to Maui, brought me a beautiful journal to write about my hospital stay. Bill, a friend I knew from California who was now living in Maui with his wife, and who was a swimmer, too, came by just to check in on me. He added yet another fin to my bookcase altar for the shark. The fins were multiplying.

The most unusual happenings of all were the phone calls and emails from people I hadn't heard from in a half a century from my elementary school in New Jersey. These friends had heard about me from television reports and radio interviews that I was giving from my hospital bed. That was one of the things that got me through. I wasn't lonely or restless then, because there were so many people out there who wanted to hear about my adventure. I was queen for a day.

It was so unlike my contact with people during most of my life where I felt like I did all the initiating—I always had to throw the party. There were people from elementary school who lived five thousand miles away on the East Coast who were just dying to talk to me about my experience. Let's face it: a human being was not often eaten by an animal, and other people wanted to hear about it.

The time to reflect, and the slow place, helped me to piece together some puzzles left over from my childhood traumas. Like why did I have such a tense relationship in elementary school with Betty? Or why did Champ seem so uninterested in me when I followed him around like a puppy in seventh grade? In their effort to hear my story, that they could hardly fathom, I was able to use my years of psychological training to extract from them who they were then, how they saw me, and what they had become. Why had I felt so small, anxious, and excluded in school? What I discovered was that they were having problems at home, just like me. It filled a small hole in my psyche that I'd long wondered about.

The most surprising phone call came from Larry King's producer, who asked me to be on *Shark Week* on CNN that August. I'd seen the special Shark Week show several years before on television. It was a panel of three or four people discussing their experiences of being attacked by a shark. It never crossed my mind in my momentarily stopping to watch the show while channel surfing that I would ever be a candidate for Shark Week. However, after spending thirty years traveling around the country on book tours and consulting jobs, going to New York to be on TV was the last thing I wanted to do when I got released.

"We'll send a limo for you," the producer said. "We'll drive you to the airport in San Francisco and pick you up in a limo at JFK. Then we'll drive you in a stretch limo to your luxurious suite at the finest hotel in the city overlooking Central Park."

I snickered. I thought to myself that they must have thought I had never been out of Maui. The idea of traveling made me feel empty and anxious with what now was becoming a very private experience.

When I told Jake, he said, "You must use it as a platform to sell the books you've written — and don't forget to talk about all your paintings you've exhibited."

"My books have nothing to do with sharks, and I paint for myself. I've already had a career, Besides, I didn't have the energy or the desire to hop on a plane and travel five thousand miles."

There was something about that way of thinking that I found opportunistic and transparent. I'd had a long career, and I didn't want to be the poster girl for a shark attack. That was one thing I knew deep down in my bones — it just didn't feel right.

The attack was something that had happened. There was a randomness to it, but for me there was a deep meaning in it despite the fact that I really wasn't able to connect the dots quite yet.

Ron feigned jealousy. "When I had my open heart surgery, I didn't get this kind of publicity, but I turn on the television each night back at the condo, and there you are — front and center."

"You never worried when you woke up each morning, filled with anxiety that I'd get eaten by a shark. Why didn't you worry about me?" I countered lamely.

Ron had told me that he and the homeless man, who went by the name Ariel, had talked on the beach after the attack and in the days that followed, exchanged phone numbers, and had several visits at the condo. Thursday afternoon, Ariel walked into my hospital room alone, with a bottle of blue water.

He said, "I came to see how you are doing. I brought this for you."

He handed me a photograph of a lotus flower in a large, gilded frame. It must have cost him a small fortune.

"The lotus flower is associated with rebirth. This is a consequence of it supposedly retracting into the water at night, and emerging afresh from a murky pond in the sun the next day. The Egyptians associated the lotus flower with the sun, which also disappeared in the night, only to re-emerge in the morning. Therefore, the lotus came to symbolize the sun, and re-creation."

Ariel told me that he'd been born and raised in the Bronx, sustained injuries in Vietnam, never graduated high school, and ended up in Hawaii, where he'd been ever since. He lived out of his van and sometimes stayed with his young girlfriend who had two small children from a previous relationship.

I was amazed at his presence in my room. I had forgotten about him in the trauma of the events after I'd gotten to the hospital. He looked exactly the same as he had been on the beach before and after the shark attack: bedraggled, Rastafarian hair hanging down to his waist, and a wrinkled, sun damaged face. I was puzzled as to why he would come and see me. I noticed things about him that I hadn't seen on the beach: He looked decidedly like a down-and-outer in this sterile hospital setting. His teeth were gray and yellow. Many were missing. His unkempt hair looked unwashed and matted, and he had a frail and emaciated look about him — yet his eyes were intensely blue and penetrating when he looked right at me. He was so earnest. My heart opened.

He — like so many other people who called or contacted Ron to find out how I was — was concerned about me. It felt like these people were holding me in an unseen way.

This brought a decidedly strange feeling. There was a safety net under me. People were thinking about me, praying for me. For the first time in my life, I didn't feel like I was coping alone. Was it the shark energy — the Shakti Pathi that the kahuna talked about? I'd never felt so filled with this kind of faith before.

Ariel continued, "The lotus is associated with rebirth. It is no surprise that the lotus flower is also associated with death, and the famous Egyptian book of the dead is known to include spells that can transform a person into a lotus — thus allowing for resurrection."

Maybe because I came from the East Coast, where people are trained to be wary, or maybe it was the rather rocky childhood I had, with spotty moments of trust, but I didn't know what to do with this kind of attention and frontal New Age assault. I mean, he did save my life — well, my emotional life, so to speak, because he knew how to soothe me and help me manage my anxiety on the beach. So I just listened and tried to appreciate his reverence and concern.

Most of my life, people have underestimated me. I had to fight to be noticed — or so it felt. I wondered in those days in the hospital what it felt like to be Princess Diana, Gloria Vanderbilt, or someone else who was born into "specialhood." They must take it for granted that people just can't wait to see them, talk to them, and listen to them for endless hours. People like me, and many others in the human race born with little or no access to this "specialhood," had to constantly find ways to get recognition. We did things to be noticed — whether overachieving or just trying to set ourselves apart.

And what was it that everyone wanted from me? Didn't they know that I was just in the wrong place at the wrong time? I felt like an imposter.

Ron walked in just then. He greeted Ariel and said, "Hey, what's that blue water?"

"I got it from a hidden creek upcountry, and I'm leaving it for your wife to drink. It will help her mend, because it's special water from a healing stream."

Even on my worst days, I would not touch a bottle of blue water, but I wanted to let him know how grateful I was that he had helped me.

"Thank you so much for helping me out on the beach, and for saying such kind words to the reporters about me in the newspapers," I said. That unsettling feeling came back as he reached out and touched my face. I couldn't help but feel worlds and realities apart from this man. I couldn't get past those eyes and the smile that made me feel uncomfortable. I hated that I felt this way because he had given me so much at a critical moment. He helped me endure my pain until the paramedics came.

Ron put his hand on Ariel's shoulder and thanked him. I never expected to see him again.

Later that morning, Doogie Howser walked in unexpectedly. He pulled up a chair in a very intentional way and set it down hard by the side of my bed. He straddled it.

"I think you are out of the woods. Your leg is healing nicely. You didn't get an infection or drop foot, so you don't require amputation, but you need to be careful going forward." Then he paused. Although I was greatly relieved to hear his decision, I had been uncertain at times; yet I had also felt a healing going on deep inside me.

"It's time for you to go," he said abruptly.

"Where?" I wasn't sure at first what he was referring to. I was just getting settled and enjoying my brief hospital vacation-filled days. I was still filled with drugs, and now I was luxuriating in the benefits of someone else making and serving meals. They were far from gourmet, but I was getting used to gumming the soft hospital food and all the red Jello I could eat. Besides, it seemed like I must be losing some weight. From my way of thinking, that was always a good thing.

"I knew my insurance would finally run out after five days."

He ignored my joke and told me he'd get things rolling and stop back soon.

I might have forgotten to mention that in the preceding days, I had gingerly slipped out of bed with a cast up to my knee, trailed by a metal contraption with two lactate ringer bags hanging from the device running solution into my forearms. My Jamoca Almond Fudge ice cream was in the nurses' lunchroom freezer, and I was enjoying my newfound celebrity. I had my cell phone, my ice cream, and my "me time." So this became my vacation—but I was adaptable, after all. Besides, I was getting a lot of unexpected attention. Did I forget to mention there was no snoring husband in the bed beside me for those four days? Long marriages are complex.

Even before the attack, I noticed that I had fewer shock absorbers to cushion me against life's slings and arrows. One minor miss during the day, and there was no easy bounce back. Now, after several days in the hospital, my body began to feel the weight of gravity again, although my right leg still felt missing in action. Perhaps this was because it was numb with painkillers and antibiotics. It seemed like after the operation, my body had shut down from the terror of the attack and the invasiveness of the four-hour surgery. About three in the afternoon every day, my brain began to unravel. I heard a cranky voice inside my head that said, be careful where you place your feet. I held my body like I would hold a baby kitten—delicately, and with care. Uncertainty was becoming a permanent condition.

Associated Press continued reporting my progress and carpeting the nation with the sensational news of a shark attack. New people from all over the country were calling and emailing me. Some I knew, and some I didn't. Then there was social media. Photos pulled from the newspaper and ones that the sly lookie-loos had taken on the beach while I was waiting for the paramedics appeared on Facebook and on some websites devoted to the misfortune of tourists who fall prey to predators in the water.

One call I got was from my friend Sherry back in Marin.

"I saw you on television. You made headlines in the *Independent Journal*. I couldn't believe it was you! Then I thought, I should call some of her friends and ask them about her. But it occurred to me that I am your friend. So here I am, calling you directly. How the hell are you?"

We both chuckled. I remember feeling the weight of obligation in making those kinds of calls when friends landed in the hospital, my not wanting to hear any bad news and not knowing what to say.

I appealed to her softer side. I described how I was bandaged up.

"We learned how to do that in nursing school," Sharon said.

"That sounds like fun. After I'm well, I'm thinking of going back to school to study nursing. This experience has been incredible," I said.

"But you gotta understand, wound healing and bandaging with the sticky tape are electives! Bandaging is only a small part of nursing. You'd have to study physiology and chemistry first."

I knew I sounded deranged, thinking that I could make a career in nursing at my age just because I was enamored with self-sticking bandages. I was still certifiable, but that didn't stop me.

"You are on so many Facebook posts, it's incredible."

I knew I was pretty visible online. Her comment made me feel happy because I hadn't disappeared out of the sight of my virtual Facebook friends.

That was followed by a strange call from a boyfriend named Terry I had dated as a junior in high school. At the time, he was a freshman at Ryder College. It harkened back to another time when I was waiting for my life to begin.

After all the niceties and explanations of how he found me on LinkedIn, Facebook, and headlines in the paper in New Jersey, he told me that he had been diagnosed with stage four esophageal cancer.

Despite that, he still sounded like the old Terry I knew. It was all I could do to not lapse into some old version of myself; yet, the old version came back so easily: softer, flirty, younger. I felt like a chameleon.

"I never thought you were going to make a big splash — no pun intended," he said. "You were into boys and clothes."

I thought he was going to ask about the shark attack, but he didn't.

"I saw you went on to get a doctorate in psychology, you wrote books, and you're an exhibiting artist — who knew?" he said in that East Coast way of not judging you but judging you at the same time. You were judged not on who you were, but by what you had done. And if you had made a good marriage.

My mild pleasure at receiving his call plummeted.

That was when Doogie Howser walked back in. I let Terry know and asked him to call again. He never did. Either he died right after that or he'd remembered why we disappeared out of each other's lives. I certainly had.

"We have the discharge papers. Call your husband and let's get things rolling."

I had learned a thing or two about hospital discharges over the years. It either takes forever, or you're pushed out within seconds and suffer from whiplash.

A nurse came in and put a black, knee-high boot with Velcro straps on me that had to be pulled tight. Then Doogie went over the instructions for my follow-up appointment. In moments, a half a dozen official papers were put before me on a clipboard. Without reading the fine print (who ever does?) I scribbled my signature and handed them back.

"You have to be careful and change your bandage every day so your wounds don't get infected. A large percentage of patients are back here within a week and have to be hospitalized again because they don't wash the wound and put clean bandages on it every day."

The nurse packed rolls of my favorite sticky tape and ointment into a plastic shopping bag and handed it to me. Now I had my own medical repair kit. I could get to be a nurse even without chemistry and physiology.

Wes and Natalie arrived with Ron to help me pack up all the things I'd collected during my stay. I'd collected so much stuff: fins, journals, magazines, get well cards, and a shopping bag filled with drugs and bandages.

Suddenly, the door opened and two young people rushed in. Each was carrying a package.

"We saw your picture and story in the paper," said the guy, who looked like a surfer dude.

The blonde-haired girl beside him blurted out, "Yeah, the Maui Dive Shop crew brought you something from our store. We hope you like it and you'll go back into the ocean soon. "

They pulled out new fins, a new mask, and a snorkel from the package.

"We also brought you a Maui Dive Shop T-shirt," said the girl. She held up a huge cotton T-shirt to her chest, mugged, smiled, and danced around in a tight circle with it before dropping it onto my bed.

After several days of quiet and healing, the room was now filled with people and noise. That old feeling of being overwhelmed and anxious began to creep in, but I was grateful that these new people, whom I didn't know, had brought me gifts from Maui Dive Shop so that once I had recovered I would have a new set of water sport gear. In fact, I was anxious to start moving and get out of the hospital that day.

21. The Gardener

WHEN WE RENTED A CONDO prior to the shark attack, we weren't told about the hammering and construction going on next door. Ron told me that while I was in the hospital, he was looking for another place for us to stay on the island. He called friends, stopped people on the street, and walked around the complex asking if anyone knew of any empty places to put us up. Ron had the ability to talk to anyone, unsolicited, about anything. I've never met anyone else who seemed so at home in the world.

"My wife — she's the one who was attacked by the shark last week...," he'd start, and that was all he'd have to say. Maui was like any small town, and everyone knew about the shark attack, so many people were ready to help. A couple from Vancouver came forth and offered us their gazillion dollar-a-night condo for a price we could afford.

Suddenly, we were moving into a mansion of a condo with air conditioning, three bedrooms, two and a half baths, Wi-Fi, Bluetooth, and a dead-on view of the ocean. Do I need to go on? Sometimes misfortune has its benefits.

The condo had recently been remodeled, and the smell of new paint and new carpet were like perfume to me. I love the smell of new. I was on my way home.

In such a short period of vacation time, we'd collected so much junk: a refrigerator and freezer's worth of food, water sport toys, suitcases filled with clothes, and books amassed along the way. It always amazed me how stuff seemed drawn to me, like steel filings to a magnet, and I could almost hear the sound of magnetic attraction: *thuf, thuf, thuf* as it flew from its place of origin into my hand, or bag, or home — and yet, how difficult it was to throw stuff out. It was like stuff created its own mysterious emotional bond and wouldn't let go. Wherever I was staying, I'd arrive back home with two or three bags of stuff — anything — and each morning, I'd start afresh, leaving empty-handed again only to fill up once more by the end of the day. Lots of in basket, no out basket.

I hadn't recovered sufficiently to pack up. My energy waned unpredict-ably — and even more than a year later, Ron himself was still recovering from open-heart surgery, and he tired easily. Gina showed up with her husband's truck, and within twenty minutes she had single-handedly hoisted all our stuff into the pickup, driven it to our new place up the hill, unpacked it, and was gone.

The next morning out of the hospital as I rested in bed, still kind of dopey from the drugs they'd given me upon discharge, I was mesmerized by the sun streaming into the bedroom, creating a rich patina of light yellow on the walls. I hobbled into the great room — the big, open area of kitchen, dining area and living room. I ran my hands over the terra-cotta striated-granite kitchen counter tops, sat on the newly upholstered bar stool that faced into the living room while I focused on the grand fireplace at the far end of the room. Hoisting my leg up onto the adjacent bar stool, I gazed at my black, foot-to-knee boot over the white cast. Then I went into the guest bathroom and explored the deep bathtub. I ran the warm water, clumsily undressed, and sat on the edge of the tub. I stepped into a plastic garbage bag that I tied at the top of my thigh to protect my cast, mindful that I could easily kill myself doing this alone. Knowing that I should probably wait for Ron to help me, I stepped gingerly into the warm water — my first real bath since before the attack. I positioned my body horizontally across the tub so that my tush and torso were in the tub while my leg dangled out of the water, and I surrendered to the familiar weightlessness of water. I had missed that feeling of comfort and effortlessness that floating in the ocean provided. It made me think of all the ways I could change my current state of mind. The list was impressive as I lay there reflecting: dark chocolate, my first cup of coffee in the morning, a walk in the hills near home, a hot bath — and swimming, of course. But I had to hold off on that one for awhile. I was so grateful to be out of the hospital, and looking forward to the follow-up appointment in a few days with the surgeon who would give me the okay to return home.

Ron was jogging on the beach that morning, so after the bath I decided to go outside and look around at our new surroundings. I dressed in a loose fitting, pullover cotton dress and hobbled over to the front door, walked outside, and admired the pikake and pink plumeria planted below me on the ground floor. Suddenly, a gust of wind came up and slammed the door closed. I turned to go back inside when I realized that I had locked myself out of the condo.

I sat down on the top stair in a daze, watching how a spotted dove alighted on the railing near the bougainvillea that climbed up the side of the adjacent condo. My mind was slipping again. My body carried a knowing more than my mind — a sensation came over me slowly, like something important was happening. There was a new quality to everything around me. Things were sharper and brighter, and the air amplified sounds. Right before me was a red cardinal. I was pleasantly carried along, and I reflected on how my mom loved cardinals. Every time they arrived in the spring, she called me from wherever I was and inevitably said, "My cardinal is back. It's going to be a wonderful year."

Now, outside the condo, I was unlike the way I usually would be — anxious and irritated at my own witlessness. My mishap didn't bother me. I felt like I was floating. I wondered what would happen next. I felt both like a stranger to myself, and more deeply myself than I had been a week before. I had lived most of my life encased in so much anxiety that I had missed so many moments to feel my aliveness, as I did right now. Where would I be, and what would I be doing, if I had trusted myself in every moment, rather than drumming up worry and anxiety?

I sat and listened to the morning sounds of the apapane and the amakihi birds on the branches of a nearby tree. I didn't see a soul for about two hours and was amazed at my lack of agitation and self-criticism that was baked into my personality. Everyone was probably at the beach by now. Then I heard the putt-putt of a golf cart as it came around the corner of the building, and there was Jorge, the gardener.

I knew that he didn't know me, at least by name, but I'd seen him many times traveling on the paths and lanes that led down to the beach or across the property. I must have looked like all the other tourists to him, and I doubted if he had ever really noticed me. I had observed him from afar before the attack because of how the cardinals flocked after his golf cart. As he came closer and stopped in front of me and broke into a broad smile, I saw his familiar, sun-weathered face. He was very earthy-looking, and my heart softened.

"How's the leg coming?" he asked. I guessed he was another person who knew about the attack, but then why shouldn't he? He rode around the property weeding, planting, and pruning every day, and was always talking to people. He wore a wide straw hat, and his broad shoulders carried a cross-body messenger bag filled with birdseed. He was a handsome, caramel-colored man who had an ageless, outdoor quality.

"Not bad. Those cardinals sure like you." Now I understood why they followed him each day when I saw him driving down to the beach. He nodded and looked behind to see a half a dozen flittering around the back of his cart, vying for the seeds.

"Locked out, eh?" he said. "I'll see if I can get a key and come back and let you in."

So there, I thought to myself as he started the engine again and moved slowly down the path. This is what happened when I just watched and waited without jumping into worry or action. Not that I was in any shape to "jump" into anything.

He came back twenty minutes later with a key to let me back in. We had a brief conversation about the bird sounds I heard.

"You know that those cardinals sound like a rusty swing set," I said.

He laughed, "I hope you get a chance to hear the 'I' iwi!" He mimicked the bird sound. He gave me a warm smile, his cart sputtered upon starting, and he slowly drove away.

An hour later, Ron wandered up the path and came inside with Ariel, the guy who had helped me on the beach.

I ran into Ariel. I hope you don't mind if he comes for lunch." Little did Ariel know that I had poured the blue water down the toilet back at the hospital after a long conversation with Ron.

"Why don't you like him?" Ron asked after Ariel left my hospital room and I'd poured out the water and flushed. "He's a soulful guy. I want to help him out—after all, he helped save your life."

"As a woman, I'm a little frightened of him. I can't explain it. I wouldn't like to be in a car alone with him."

I explained to Ron that there are things that a woman feels about being vulnerable and alone with certain men that other men don't feel. Ron understood.

There was the toothless, greasy-haired, ageless man yet again. He went to hug me, and I let him. All of a sudden, I wasn't feeling very generous, though. Only moments before, I had been ready to hop into Jorge's golf cart and spend the day with him, riding around and watching, listening, and feeding the birds. I didn't know Ariel any better than I knew Jorge. Ariel had been nothing but kind, yet I felt wary of him. At times, I saw a strange, beatific smile come across his face like someone who had done too many drugs. That also frightened me. Ron started to make a salad, and asked Ariel to tell us about himself and what it was like living on the beach.

"I live on the beach when the weather is good, but I live in my van when it gets cold. Cold in Maui is about fifty degrees, but because it's on the ocean it can get very raw at times. When I came back from Vietnam, I couldn't handle the mainland, so I came here to chill out."

I could just imagine how difficult his life must have been. And yet he was still willing to come to my rescue. My heart began to open to him. He had had such a hard time, Ron generously wanted him to know how glad we were that he had helped me. I was grateful that Ron took the lead, because I was still in no shape to show him my thanks. While we ate our salads, in the back of my mind, I was focused on waiting for the phone to ring—I was expecting a call from Dr. Toma with the final lab results. If I was cleared of any residual infections, I could get a cast on my foot and permission to travel home. I needed a doctor's okay to leave the island and board a plane.

The afternoon was slowly ebbing into another amazing sunset, and Dr. Toma still hadn't called. Typical of how most people operated on Maui time. But I was dealing with a doctor's office, not a nail salon.

I tried every day for five days to reach him, but he didn't pick up.

Sometimes I tried several times a day. We called the hospital, but no one there knew where he was. Some didn't even know who he was. How could a doctor who spent hours operating on your leg be a mysterious stranger to a hospital? Had he just wandered in off the street to perform this operation? Ron and I alternately laughed and worried about this turn of events. How could a doctor have disappeared off the island?

I called Wes, Natalie, and Jake. Since Dr. Toma had recently arrived, no one knew much about him. I called the hospital Each time a different story—he had gone off island (a nice turn of a phrase for going back to Massachusetts), he had never been at the hospital, his office had closed down.

I was frantic. There were no other orthopedic surgeons on Maui. He knew my history.

Ron followed my lead. As worriers, the worst thing for each of us to have done was to marry another worrier. When I got crazy with panic, he said things like, "If you think that's bad, how about this?" And then he escalated it to an even higher level of a nuclear emotional bomb. Until neither one of us could think clearly.

Finally, on day six, I reached the doctor's office.

A strange female voice answered the phone.

"Aloha, Dr. Toma's office," the voice said.

I vented first. "How can a doctor disappear? I've been trying to call for days. Doesn't he answer his phone?"

"He was surfing on the other side of the island with no cell phone coverage," the woman said. "I'm his receptionist and his wife. We can set up an appointment."

The next day Ron and I found his tiny office in a clapboard house in a run-down side of town in Wailuku. A woman who I thought must have been his nurse answered the door.

"I'm sorry for the delay." He came out from a back room and introduced his wife and nurse, Nina, who ushered me into the examining room where I lay down on the padded table.

He entered the room but said nothing. In one thrust of an arm, using his hand and full body strength, he ripped the truss off my leg. He had "blindsided" me, and it was excruciatingly painful. My feelings were hurt, but my leg also ached from his pulling on the thick fishing line that held my flesh together in the heavy bandage. I would have been sobbing like a baby if I weren't the center of attention. It flashed across my mind that a shark attack victim needed to appear stoic. His nurse-wife aided him silently, while calming me by rubbing my hand in hers.

My naked leg seemed thinner than it had been before, and where there was once smooth skin, there was now a hairline scar that started at my big toe, disappeared around my ankle, and then ran up the side of my calf.

"That will disappear over time."

"Pretty good for someone who only worked on an eel bite before,"

"You're lucky I practiced on an eel. Pretty good for my second operation on sea creatures, I'd say," he shot back.

No bedside manner.

No apology for being snarky.

By that time, I knew I had better keep my mouth shut.

He walked out, leaving me with Nina. She looked like a character out of a Louisa May Alcott novel. Of course, they had come from Massachusetts recently—it was Emily Dickinson country, and she was a Massachusetts woman. Her hair was long, straight, and parted in the middle—very heroine like. She had that thin, pretty look with a perfect no-hips body, the kind I'd always wished I'd gotten when hips were given out. As my internal dialog babbled on, he entered the room again.

"Your tests look good—you are good to go," he told me. "Stay out of the water for several months, but you must start getting some exercise to build up your strength again."

Sitting in the rental car on the ride back to the condo, braving the tourist gridlock at that hour, I realized this crisis was never going to make me younger, tougher, stronger, or more relevant. I was still wondering why this had happened to me. Was being in the wrong place at the wrong time a real explanation? It wasn't for me. I want to find meaning in all the episodes in my life — connecting the dots, looking for synchronicity. Maybe I couldn't count on my crisis connecting me to some spiritual fork in the road that would inform my life. As I looked out the window, I pondered about the mystery: even the most mundane and the most spectacular moments of my existence could be inhabited by hidden complexity and enigmatic wonder.

22. Time for Reflection

MAUI HAD NO HARD EDGES. In life, things could change imperceptibly, or you could be quickly blindsided. But things always changed. The closer I was to nature, the more clearly I could see it.

Maui had seemed exempt from the catastrophes that happened in the rest of the world. It was a dreamy paradise to tourists and inhabitants alike. Sure, the island had a rare volcanic eruption or an infrequent hurricane, but the inhabitants saw themselves as untouched by the problems of the mainland. Some of my friends seemed to be legends in their own minds, until they had to take stock of food, water, and shelter, just in case the Armageddon really happened.

Several years before, our group of friends joined forces with the county and the state to take inventory of their needs in a crisis. They arrived at the startling realization that the state of Hawaii had only about three days' worth of drinkable water, and that most foods vital to survival were shipped in and had to be distributed from the port in Honolulu, on Oahu. The people of Maui were indeed remote from the mainland.

Some years later, North Korea landed a test missile just short of the islands. That shocked our friends into silence and out of their false security and superiority: The-We-Live-in-Paradise monologue ended abruptly. Ron and I saw Maui as our second home, but Marin was our real home.

Indeed, our friends lived in a paradise, despite the fact that traffic had increased exponentially as many condos were going up since we started visiting. Property taxes had shot up and become exorbitant for the older inhabitants of the island. Unable to pay their taxes, they sold to Midwesterners or investors from Japan or China. Large McMansions intruded upon older cottages on the water, and later changed the shorelines of Makena and Wailea. And, finally, the processing and burning of sugarcane increased pollution to alarming high levels, causing respiratory problems for many island dwellers and tourists alike.

By 2006, the year before my attack, our friends didn't want to drive down Haleakala Highway at night because of the dramatic increase in head-on collisions due to crystal meth use by teenagers.

I noticed that the water by the hotels had become full of sewage that washed out of the culverts draining into the ocean: tampons, dirty diapers, six-pack holders, and bottle caps. And finally, the schools of fish that inhabited that part of the island were becoming scarce. My Christmas Wrasses were gone, and there were fewer Moorish Idols. Della, Marvin's wife, was diagnosed with cancer in 2008 and died a year later. Buzzy died of melanoma that same year.

⌒

Late that afternoon and into the night in the condo as I was recovering, I uncovered a new and deeper inner landscape. I found myself in my own prison of self-recrimination and shame. I met all the people from the past with whom I harbored disappointments or felt slighted by. They were my prison guards. I may not have seen or spoken to them in years, but at that hour when the night shift had settled in, they visited me with questions that remained unanswered. Just as any shred of forgiveness begged to be teased out, I was carried off down the river of shame and regret despite all the therapy, self-help books, and comforting friends who asserted, "Well, shit happens." I began blaming myself for the shark attack — for being in the wrong place, at the wrong time, and not being aware.

The worst was over. I had time for reflection in the condo, and — depending on the content that I reflected upon — that reflection could either produce good feelings, or bad feelings. I realized that I had spent so much of much of my life looking ahead that often I wasn't present, thinking about my future.

While Ron sat at the table on the lanai that night, trying to book us a flight home with our non-refundable, time limited, super saver tickets, wheeling and dealing with agents, I overheard snippets of the conversation from the bedroom and made a list of all my losses. Call me perverse. It actually made me feel better as I sat up in bed recovering. I called it *The Department of Things I Can't Control*. It was my way back to health — understanding this random act of attack.

I had lost my mom and dad, and my childbearing years were over. Ron had taken a big hit with his heart surgery episode — and as his caregiver, so did I. Although I didn't know it at the time, there were signs that friends' marriages and relationships were coming undone. The foreshadowing of change loomed large in each couple's life. It was like a slow-moving train that reached its destination shortly after the shark attack.

I reflected on some things that definitely wouldn't happen in the future: we wouldn't have children, we wouldn't own another house, we wouldn't travel to distant places, and we wouldn't have any more brilliant career plans. How did each of us ever have the energy to have a successful consulting business for so many years? How did I ever find the time and imagination to write four books, or exhibit my paintings?

It struck me that some of the people around me were the age deniers. They professed to know how to stay young and wrote books about the joys of aging, but I knew these were only half-truths.

It was that question of my age that the reporter made after the shark attack, of all the other comments and questions that stuck with me and disturbed me the most. It was a confrontation on a deep level: that I was a legend in my own mind, just like my Maui friends. I was an aging woman, even an old woman. That was how strangers saw me. I needed to face it.

The next time Gina came over to visit me at the condo, I asked her — what was so joyful about aging? In order to placate me that afternoon, we drew up a list of all the good and bad things about aging. Little of it satisfied me.

But even in the grand condo, I couldn't sleep at night. When I tried to sleep, I feared closing my eyes. I lay on my belly on the floor, my arms out over my head, and hands flattened on the floor, palms down. I imagined I was in the water doing the dead man's float — swimming and almost sleeping, but not quite. At times I felt like I was drowning. Finally, this was the way I fell asleep night after night. I was holding onto something solid for dear life, so that I didn't float away. I could not bring myself to tuck away the shark episode — even the painful parts — because I came out alive.

Ron finally got us a flight out at the end of the week. Each morning that week I woke up to sunlight and cardinals singing their song. I imagined that the shark had imbued me with a strange Shakti Pathi — a form of energy.

At night, everything was fraught with danger, during the day, I was anxious. I woke up in the middle of the night because I thought I heard the walls breathing.

The episode was sinking in. *This really happened to me? What if something else happens to Ron and me?* We had built a life together. We'd done it accumulating life experiences; but life could be hurtful, untrustworthy, hard, scary, and time was always ticking on. Because of this life-and-death experience, sometimes now I felt like I was behind a glass barrier that separated me from other people. I knew something, I had experienced something that they could only imagine and could never understand.

It was a difficult period, but was always an outrageously bright, sunny day in paradise. Inside, I was on edge.

Each night slipped again into a sunlight-flooded day. The sky had never seemed so clear, or the air so clean and moist. The day had all its distractions. I felt like I was on mescaline—shark mescaline. During the day I never felt so good to be alive. I thought, this must be what it feels like to live without fear or depression. But when nights came, I was frightened and the turmoil of meaning began again.

A psychiatrist friend of Ron's told him I had some form of PTSD from the shark attack.

"We all have PTSD," I responded. "Life is difficult. Each moment is a decision: the choice to leave home, to stop at the market for a few things, or to pass a car in the left lane—a split-second decision could end your life. "

I knew I was punting—trying this on for size for the first time—but I was raw and sleep deprived.

"Oh, so every little mistake in judgement could end your life?" Ron said. We laughed in the face of these half-truths. The narrative of each life has curves, sheer drop offs, hairpin turns—life was an accumulation of experiences until you swerved.

23. Saying Goodbye

WE HAD A FEW MORE DAYS on Maui before we left. I was withdrawing into my shell, so Ron suggested a drive upcountry to visit the volcano.

"I'm tired of you telling me that the walls are closing in on you," he said.

I was grateful to get out of the condo. It changed my mood.

As we drove down Pu'unene Road past the dilapidated sugar mill, up ahead was the square, Pepto-Bismol-pink cinderblock building in the middle of a huge vacant field. We drove up Pulehu Road to Omaopio Road, and through the acres and acres of sugarcane and pineapple. We weren't going up the Haleakala Highway, but towards Keokea and Wes and Natalie's house.

Ron turned off the road onto a rutted dirt road that climbed the flank of the volcano, along an unmarked trail, and then another rough dirt road. Ron kept inching along, certain he knew where he was going.

I thought someone told me that there was a monastery up here that some guy built to honor his guru from India," he told me.

"I thought we were going to the volcano?"

"After this," he said.

We were lost, of course. How could we be lost in the middle of the day? On a mountaintop on a small island? With a three-hundred-and-sixty-degree view around us?

"Isn't the right thing just to head back down?" I asked..

There was a network of one-lane, red clay roads behind us and before us. It could take us hours before we could get down and find our way back. Suddenly, I saw a lanky man about our age coming towards us. He didn't seem particularly friendly. I waved, trying to be cheerful.

Ron stopped the engine and hopped out.

"We're looking for a temple our friend Jake told us about. The guy we are looking for goes by the name Jeff Riggs. Can you help us?"

The guy seemed to soften and recognized Jake's name. He introduced himself as Jeff. He was indeed the guy Ron had been told about.

"It's a little way up, over the top of that ridge ahead," Jeff said.

Ron asked him to hop in the car with us and take us to the temple he had built.

Sure enough, a short distance ahead over the next rise was a terra cotta clay temple in the middle of nowhere—and I mean nowhere—that looked like it was right out of Poona, India. Well, pictures of India, because I'd never actually been there. Jeff ushered us inside.

As we sat on cushions, Jeff told us about how he came to Maui to get away from all the noise in the world. He lived as caretaker of this temple until his guru could join him from India.

"When is he coming?" I asked. Leave it to me—full frontal.

Jeff took a very long pause before he spoke.

"I've spent the last fifteen years building this temple as a dedication to my guru, who has made me into a better person." Jeff then revealed his journey from boyhood, and his hardscrabble life that landed him in prison for drugs.

"I decided that when I got out of prison, I was going to India and change myself by prayer and meditation into a better human being. That was my goal, and I did it. After several years in India my guru told me to go to Maui and build him a temple. He said he would come here and live in the temple. My guru says he is coming soon. But he is very old now, and I'm not sure he can make the trip."

I reflected on how each person makes a life for themselves in one way or another.

That afternoon we drank chai. I told him about the shark attack.

After I was done, and the golden shadows cast by the sun moved steadily towards the horizon, I knew we'd better find our way down the mountain before dark.

He suddenly turned to me and said, "You wanted this in your life, didn't you?"

I was silent. How could I have wanted this encounter with a shark? I noticed myself becoming defensive, but I knew there was wisdom in what he was asking. I paused. There must have been some truth in the question. I wanted to answer him honestly because he seemed like a person who had a profound understanding of unseen things. Why else spend years of his life in prayer and solitude, building a temple to his guru? I spoke in a whisper, because maybe I didn't want to hear what I was about to say:

"I was becoming a shell. I'd lost touch with myself along the way, but I didn't know how deep it was at the time or how to get back to myself. Then the shark appeared. It woke me up. I needed a wake-up call. I had to pull myself out of that dark pit."

24. Mother Maui

WE DROVE HOME SILENTLY, and I thought about what Jeff had asked me.

The Shark Attack was an event that divided my life into a before and after scenario.

Things changed in a blink.

Before it, I was a bit of a legend in my own mind—that's why I saw this in others. After all, projection is autobiographical. Now I had to accept that I was an aging woman. Yet, in the aging process, I had built an emotional muscle I never thought I had.

Still, I did have a community of younger selves who continued to inform me. The twenty-year old who doggedly pursued men that I thought could rescue me. The young woman who recklessly sought adventure, the adult who grew in focus and intention, the middle-aged woman who buried two parents, the wife who became a caregiver to her recovering husband, and the woman who survived a shark attack. All these women were still me.

I met the shark attack alone, and I made the right choices. I was lucky. I survived an unprecedented crisis. I had been forever altered by a full frontal brush with death.

The tide was going out. The ocean was exhaling.

Wes had said that you went from A to Z on Maui. No matter where you began on the island and which direction you headed your car, you ended up back where you started by nightfall. Everyone was friendly and ebullient. You'd have to be, or you'd burn out your friends. How could you be depressed with a vast blue sky, a beach, and an expansive ocean before you? But living in paradise had its costs. It was a metaphor for having a relationship with yourself: time slowed down, beauty was everywhere, and there was nowhere to go. You were thrust back into yourself.

The last day on the island, a pearlescent-green hummingbird flew into our windowpane. Horrified, I picked the bird up off the ground and put him under the mango tree. The bird's accident made as much sense as being attacked by an eighteen-foot tiger shark.

Somehow, Ron and I had begun to break through the illusion that we might put down roots in this paradise, but the shark event opened us up to the possibility that nothing stays the same forever. It's called loss. When I think of loss, I think of death, but loss had become a grander theme than that. I not only lost, or almost lost people through death, but through the simple, inevitable, unrelenting movement of time, leaving, being left, people changing, letting go, and moving on. There was also the loss of romantic dreams, impossible expectations, illusions of safety—and the loss of my younger self. The self that could not imagine being wrinkled, vulnerable, and mortal.

And what happened to people touched by Mother Maui? I could not shake the stories of what happened to my friends: Wes wanted to leave the island and move to Thailand, where the cost of living was cheaper. But Natalie didn't want to go. As time approached, Natalie absentmindedly made a left turn into oncoming traffic on Haleakala highway, disabling her for the rest of her life. Thailand became the road not taken. And Wes was launched into his own caregiver role.

When Fuzzy and Gina met up in North Carolina several days after she helped us move into the condo, she discovered a mole on Fuzzy's arm. Eight months later, despite rounds of chemo and radiation, he died. Meanwhile, Della learned she had cervical cancer, chose not to have radiation, and died quietly in her garden in the midst of writing poetry. Flynn and Aurora got divorced—and so did several other couples. Like a house of cards, each life was collapsing. Maybe Mother Maui had embraced some, and then spit them out. Was there anyone not touched in some way by Mother Maui?

Our last night sitting outside on our lanai, my eyes filled with tears at the things I'd miss: the sound of the cardinals, the surf rolling into the shore at night, and the sweet fragrance of the morning air.

How much of life was about waiting: there was linear time—a chronology of the past, present, and future—and then there was soul time, as I'd come to realize in the hospital. Soul time was a quality that could not be measured, that came from the inside out. Part of getting acquainted with soul time for me was learning how to listen to the silence, and to recognize the pauses, the gaps, the stops, the heartbeat, and the breath.

Time molded us, yet was so malleable. Sometimes it went missing. Sometimes I had to let go of it and float to be able to survive.

Who was this new, aging woman whom I was destined to continue to know deep inside of me—the one who pulled the precious thing from the dark pit, and the one who strengthened her emotional muscles in the face of death? In every loss, there seemed to be a thread, a seed of something newly developing: when I thought of Greece, Botswana, the fear of swimming, or my caregiving of Ron. Each helped me develop a stronger emotional muscle, shocking myself into trusting my new-found strength.

The night before we finally left Maui, I listened to the waves crest and break, roaring onto the beach — the inhale and exhale of the sea. The voice of Mother Maui lulled me to sleep.

The next morning, I woke up in bed with Ron still asleep beside me. I slipped into a swimsuit and wandered out onto a soft stretch of white sand. The sky at that hour was cloudless, like every other day there. The air was already hot. The West Maui Mountains lay to my right, soaking in the heat. I looked overhead at the sky. I knew it was going to be another perfect day in paradise, and then I bent down and dipped my hands into the salt water. The patterns the surf was making on the sandy bottom became an inspiration for my next painting. I harvested well-being from the form, color, and wavy lines reflecting light like ribbons and shadows below. Tiny fish darted near the surface. I tried to memorize the pattern of light and dark as the ocean moved and swayed. I promised myself that I would capture them with oil sticks and acrylics when I got back home.

Confusion was receding, but no clarity was taking its place. There had been countless foretellings, innumerable small breaks with normalcy — the warning signs had been ever so slight. The film of what had happened was always now in my memory. Wherever I went, it would always be playing. Life's secrets were beyond analysis or understanding. I had deepened to embrace the pain, and to become more than I had been before. I knew I had been changed by my shark encounter.

For a final time, I gazed up at the West Maui Mountains, the surf surged onto the beach, and I said goodbye to my shark and to Mother Maui.

About the Author

In early May of 2007, Peller Marion, psychologist and corporate consultant, was savaged and nearly killed by an eighteen-foot, three-thousand-pound tiger shark in the waters off Kihei, Maui. After it occurred, this shark attack was a human-interest story that generated national and international attention and played out publicly on television and in newspapers. But her recovery, both physical and emotional, has been a very private process — one she chronicles in *Shark Attack and Other Mishaps*.

Peller's past includes climbing Mt. Kilimanjaro in Tanzania, racing motorcycles, and working as a Gestalt Art Therapist. She is the author of several books, including *Crisis Proof Your Career* and the novel *Searching for the G Spot*.

Since the attack, Peller has returned to the artistic life. She exhibits her watercolors and mixed media work in galleries in Marin County, California, where she lives with her husband and cat. She also teaches a bi-weekly creative writing workshop at a community college and a class on mixed media and collage at O'Hanlon Center for the Arts. She still swims, but only in swimming pools.

For more about Peller go to pellermarion.com.

CPSIA information can be obtained
at www.ICGtesting.com
Printed in the USA
FSHW022220290120
66424FS